P9-EFJ-647

*be honest—*
YOU'RE NOT THAT
INTO HIM EITHER

Also by Ian Kerner, Ph.D.

*She Comes First: The Thinking Man's Guide
to Pleasuring a Woman*

**10 ReganBooks**
**Celebrating Ten Bestselling Years**
*An Imprint of* HarperCollins*Publishers*
www.reganbooks.com

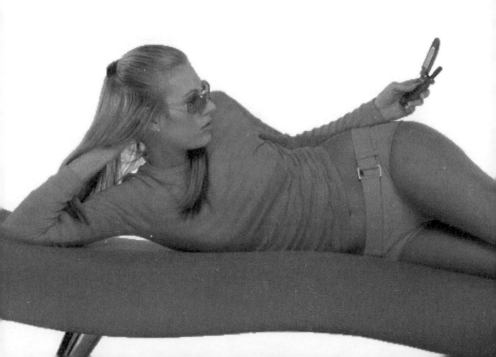

*be honest—*
# YOU'RE NOT THAT INTO HIM EITHER
## RAISE YOUR STANDARDS AND REACH FOR THE LOVE YOU DESERVE

IAN KERNER, PH.D.
Foreword by Amy Sohn

BE HONEST—YOU'RE NOT THAT INTO HIM EITHER. Copyright © 2005 by Ian Kerner, Ph.D. All rights reserved. Printed in the United States of America. No part of this book may be used or reproduced in any manner whatsoever without written permission except in the case of brief quotations embodied in critical articles and reviews. For information address HarperCollins Publishers Inc., 10 East 53rd Street, New York, NY 10022.

HarperCollins books may be purchased for educational, business, or sales promotional use. For information please write: Special Markets Department, HarperCollins Publishers Inc., 10 East 53rd Street, New York, NY 10022.

FIRST EDITION

Designed by Kate Nichols

Printed on acid-free paper

Library of Congress Cataloging-in-Publication Data has been applied for.

ISBN 0-06-081740-2

05 06 07 08 09 WBC/RRD 10 9 8 7 6 5

"To single women everywhere: Don't leave your everlasting gobstopper of love on the table. You go girls."

# contents

*foreword*

I was sitting at a bar in my Brooklyn neighborhood waiting for a guy to show up. We had been dating about two weeks, and it was one of those semidefinite plans that can only lead to heartbreak for one of the parties. He had said he'd stop by at some point, and I said I'd be getting there at 9. It was now 10:45, and I had been drinking vodka tonics slowly, fretting to the female bartender, and getting progressively more demoralized. Maybe he hadn't said he'd definitely come by. Maybe he'd said he *might,* which was a totally different thing from *would.* Maybe he said he'd do it at the end of the night and not the beginning, in which case I couldn't even be legitimately annoyed. But I knew I wasn't deaf or stupid, and I remembered very clearly what he'd said: "I'll definitely come by after work." He worked late sometimes, but not *this* late. And if he *were* working this late, he should have called.

For the past hour and a half I had been periodically lifting my cell phone off the bar and checking to see if somehow, magically, the SILENT RING button had managed to press itself. Sometimes I'd make myself stop and swear not to lift it again, and then a few minutes later I'd break down and check, like someone with OCD who's convinced they forgot to lock the door. As if that weren't enough, every fifteen minutes I would call my home machine to see if he'd called to say he wasn't coming, although I knew he had my cell phone number.

It never occurred to me to leave, not at 9:30 or even at 10:30. All I could think about was that he said he'd come, and I had to wait until he did.

After a little while I noticed that the guy next to me, a slender, older man with worn eyes, had been watching me. "Are you waiting for someone?" he finally asked.

"Yeah," I said. "I'm seeing this guy, and he said he'd stop by, and I know I look like a real idiot, but I'm really into him."

He shook his head and said, "But you're so beautiful, and you seem intelligent. Why would you do this to yourself? If he can't get his act together to come here then you're obviously way too good for him. Why are you wasting your time?"

I nodded contemplatively and then did what all girls do when struck with an insight this intense and on-target: ordered another vodka tonic and went out onto the sidewalk to see if he was coming.

This story might be less embarrassing if I could honestly say this was the first time I had ever acted like a moron over a worthless guy. But—although I cringe to admit it—over the course of my twenties there were at least a dozen guys who drove me to obsess, fret, call, not call, deconstruct, and lament to all my girl-friends. There was a guy who called me from a pay phone, ran out of quarters, and then called *five days later.* There was a film director who complained about his career slump *for an hour and a half,* without asking me a single question about myself. There was the actor who left my apartment after a hot night of make-out, saying that instead of having breakfast with me, he needed to build some shelves. Did I thank any of these guys for letting me know, in no uncertain terms, to cross them off my list? On the contrary. I logged weeks over the phone with friends trying to make sense of them, concocting any excuse that would make it possible for me to keep seeing them: He lost my phone num-ber, he lost his cell phone, he went out of town, he's going through a rough patch emotionally, he's getting over his ex-girlfriend, his divorce is making it hard for him to get close, his subway broke down, he got really busy at work, or he got hit by a truck.

One guy I really liked, a quirky documentary filmmaker named Dan, went MIA for three weeks after what I thought was a great first date, and just as I was about to give up on dating for-ever, a friend of his called to tell me Dan had gotten cancer and checked into a hospital for treatment. Instead of feeling sad I felt relieved: After dating dozens of guys who had no excuses, I'd fi-nally met someone who had one!

The most horrifying aspect of dating all these jerks was that I began to realize that I had a lot of company. I wasn't an anomaly, one neurotic Jewish girl with father issues who needed years of therapy to learn not to waste her time with ambivalent men. All of my friends were going through the same thing. When I wasn't on the phone complaining about the guy who left the country unexpectedly and never came back, I was consoling the friend who was dating a guy who asked her to leave after they slept together, or the one who had spent a romantic weekend with a guy in the country never to hear from him again, or the one losing sleep over the guy she met on the subway platform who loved her but didn't want to be monogamous. Some of their losers made *my* guys look gentlemanly.

As I talked to more and more women at parties and at work, I began to see that this was an epidemic. It seemed that thousands of college-educated, professional, high-achieving, and intelligent women were wasting hours of time on men who were treating them horribly. We were the daughters of the same 1970s feminists who believed, "A woman without a man is like a fish without a bicycle," and yet we were pining away like schoolgirls over men who shouldn't have been worth a second date. What was going on?

This is something I've been thinking about these last few years, after I finally met, fell in love with, and married a man who treated me with respect from moment one. As my life has changed, I've watched my friends. Some have gone on to meet wonderful people, while others are still logging asshole time, worried about their fertility, and afraid they'll never meet anyone they could marry.

I am not sure who is to be blamed for the unprecedented chasm between the sexes these days, for the miscommunication, dodginess, and emotional abuse, and meanness from men to women (and let's face it, from women to men). Perhaps it's broken homes; or faulty parenting; or the biological clock, which makes women so desperate for a mate that they're willing to overlook major personality flaws; or the fetishizing of casual sex in the 1990s, which tricked women into thinking they didn't have feelings; or the advances of women in the work world, which made them think they could snag a husband with the same persistence they used in the office. It could be all of these things or none. But by the time anyone figures out the reason, we will all be dead.

So I think it's time we began focusing not on the disease but the cure. The cure is simple, ancient, universally effective, and yet strangely elusive. It can be as hard to locate as the flu vaccine, but when you find it, your sense of well being sets in almost immediately. What is this magical antidote?

Pride.

No, you can't walk into a party with pride as your date and get envious looks from other women. You can't marry pride, and you can't have babies with it. You can't give pride a blow job or have online sex with it. But pride can give you orgasms, and it most definitely can lighten your mood.

If I had left that bar at 9:30, taking home no man but at least keeping my pride, I might have been able to stop dating my no-show the very next day. I could have been spared weeks of agony that prevented me from meeting thousands of wonderful guys. When I got home that night, maybe I would have read a book or taken a bath or watched TV or even lay down on the bed and cried, but I would have done so with my dignity intact.

When I finally left that bar at 11:30, wobbling home, demoralized and depressed, I was upset not because he had failed to show up but because I'd sat in a bar alone for two and a half hours waiting for him. And what I didn't realize was that after a certain point, it no longer mattered if he came because *he'd already ruined things*. As I discovered the next time I saw him, there was no joy in our eventual reunion because the dream I'd had for us was already dead. I knew he wasn't going to turn around just as I knew that his not showing up at the bar was only one of several things he had done wrong over the course of the few weeks we'd been dating.

After an amazing first date he had said he'd call the next day and didn't. He had been cagey about physical intimacy to the point where it was unclear whether he was interested in women at all. He complained constantly about his job but never asked me about my own. He invited me away for the weekend and then asked me to get the rental car myself, pick him up at work, and split the cost with him. But I didn't want to look at any of that behavior because I was too scared to interpret what that information might mean: We weren't meant to be. I was afraid to cancel the wedding planner I'd already hired in my head.

The reason pride can be so elusive for women is because it often comes hand in hand with accepting that things weren't meant to be, and accepting this can be painful, depressing, and lonely. But *the sadness fades.* All the ambivalent, shady, hot-and-cold rockers and writers and artists I dated in my twenties were guys I could laugh about a week after it ended. The recovery never took nearly as long as the months of floundering in non-relationships.

This book is about how to find your pride and use it to take action in matters of the heart. Unlike some books, it will not give you a magical formula or try to convince you that all the power lies in the hands of men. Ian Kerner is that rare man who truly loves women and wants to help them (I mean, come on. The guy wrote an entire book about giving oral sex to women). *Be Honest— You're Not That Into Him Either* is a smart and very funny guide to getting off your butt and getting back on the journey that will eventually lead you to someone who loves you and treats you well. Your mensch is out there; you just have to know how to spot him. A friend of mine once said, "Your twenties are about figuring out what you want and your thirties are about figuring out how to get it." When*ever* it happens, you do need to figure out what you want—and *don't* want—before you can have a chance of being happy. You have to stop treading water. Ian takes you through all the excuses you've been making and dismantles them one by one. In so doing, he shows you a way out of the patterns that have been making you miserable all these years.

This is not a prescriptive book, the kind that tells you to follow certain rules or that claims all men are the same so you'd better accept it and act accordingly. It is smarter, more nuanced, and more complicated. But it will tell you how to put your own needs first and begin to recognize when they're not being met—sexually or emotionally. Ian is not against casual sex, but his advice on it is sound: If you're having it you should at least be having mind-blowing orgasms. There is nothing worse than a drunken and sexually unequal one-night-stand with someone you barely know. You wake up in the morning with your tongue feeling like cotton, wondering what his name is and then remembering that you didn't even come. What is the point of casual sex if the sex part isn't any good?

Similarly, what is the point of dating someone if he's not making you feel great? Why muddle through life when you can make active choices? You wouldn't stay at a job you hated or endure a friendship that wasn't giving you something, so why use a different set of standards when it comes to men?

A few months after I told my bar no-show that I didn't want to see him any more, he called me on my cell phone. I was caught off guard, but I answered. "I just wanted to apologize for being such a freak," he said. "I didn't treat you well. I was going through a lot at work and . . ."

As he went on I shook my head. He was still wrapped up in his own drama, even now. He wanted a sympathetic ear to complain to about his emotional drama, even after we had stopped dating.

"That's OK," I said, interrupting him. "It just wasn't right. I don't resent you. I wish you all the best." And I meant it.

I hung up the phone, and then I did something that only took a second but made me feel better than I had in months: I deleted him.

*introduction:*
ARE YOU REALLY THAT
INTO HIM?

*M*en are jerks. We don't call when we say we will. We lie. We cheat on our wives and our girlfriends. We leave the toilet seat up, and we engage in a host of clichéd behaviors that modern dating guides lay out in obvious terms so you can move on with your lives. Yes, some men are jerks. But you know that because you've dated us. And you're smart enough to know that when a guy doesn't call you, it means he's not that into you.

But despite your intelligence, you've begun to operate on his terms. And who can blame you? Go on enough bad dates and your hopes of finding love are sure to diminish. You start to make adjustments, taking a realistic and pragmatic approach. You begin to settle. You know that frogs don't turn into princes, so you lower your standards enough until it gets difficult to tell the two apart. Whether out of good old-fashioned horniness, social pressure (combined with the perception that there are no good men left), or simply the dismal dating disappointments you continually face, you've lowered your standards—perhaps without even realizing it. But in doing so, you've forgotten that while he may be showing you that he's not that into you, the truth is *you were never really that into him in the first place.* Be honest. You were with him while you were waiting for something better to come along. He wasn't that great to begin with but he was better than nothing. Or was he?

You settled, and then you got stuck. Well, this book is going to help you get unstuck.

What makes me such an expert? Well, first off, I'm a man, so I am well qualified to write about male limitations (I need only look in the mirror). But in addition to my chromosomal makeup, I'm a sex therapist and I talk to women (and men) every day about their erotic and romantic issues. And what has struck me most over the past year or so is not the inability of women to read men's all-too-clear signs of relative disinterest but women's passive decisions to sleep with, date, and ultimately fall in love with men they never really liked in the first place.

Take, for instance, the "curious case of the girl in the elegant black dress."

Last fall I was giving a talk at a singles event in lower Manhattan when a stunning thirty-one-year-old blond woman stood to ask a question. Tall, attractive, and well put together, she was the picture of feminine confidence:

"I'm so fed up. I'm ready to be in a relationship but I date these guys and it's like an episode of *The Bachelor*—in the back of your mind you know there are all these other beautiful women competing for him, *and he knows you know that,* and these days waiting to have sex until the third date is almost quaint, so next thing you know, you're hooking up and wondering why he's being so standoffish and . . ."

At this point a guy in the audience shouted, "Maybe he's just not that into you," echoing the mantra of a certain book with the same title that swept bestseller lists and caused quite a stir late last year.

A smattering of laughter ensued.

"Possibly," she retorted. "But when I heard that title, you know what my first response was? 'Guess what? I was never into you either!'" she shouted. "If I really stop to think about it, I'm getting hung up on men I never wanted in the first place. And all the women I know feel the same way. We've collectively lowered our standards without even realizing it."

"So, then why are you dating these guys?" I asked.

She hesitated, then answered, "Because somehow it feels like I should be dating but there aren't that many great choices out there. And I guess I'm caught in something I can't get out of."

She thought for another moment.

"And, you know, because I like to sleep with men."

Oh, yeah, that.

Now, I'm not out to question your right to have sex if you get horny or lonely. Second-wave feminists fought for that right, and you were most likely born with it. It's no longer about ensuring your right to pursue pleasure. It's yours, sista, so use it as you see fit. But use it wisely. Think about how you wield that power and what the costs are of sleeping with guys you might not be that into. Trust me, he's getting something out of the bargain, but what are you getting?

But there's more to this than sex. The proliferation of the Rabbit vibrator tells us that women are capable of getting themselves off without having to suffer through another dreary date with yet another misfit with a Club Monaco charge card. Successful, attractive, empowered women are dating (and falling for) men who they know they're not into. This is happening every day, from New York to San Francisco and even in Ohio. It has probably already happened to you.

Part of the problem is the dating marketplace. The world is full of sensational women (trust me, I see you all the time—I'm married, not dead) but there are too few men to go around, or so it appears, and you're forced to settle. Are all the good ones taken? Of course not, but then again, they don't seem to be hanging out on your doorstep either. So, you keep sleeping with the ones you're not really into. But truth be told, it's women's sexually empowered behavior that's helping create an army of men who've come to expect that and nothing more.

Then there are the pressures of the social marketplace. Settle down and have children, it seems to say. A family? That's a great idea! You'll get right on that, after you perfect cold fusion. But it's easier said than done, especially when you cannot meet someone you want to see for a third date. And don't you live in the world of third-wave feminism? Yes, but as modern as the world may seem, certain traditions still rule the day. The pressure to get married, however, may be leading you to make some bad choices.

And all of this is what keeps the dating treadmill spinning at such a fast and constant pace that you forget to notice that you're not actually getting anywhere. You've been at this so long it seems like the reality is: Girl meets less-than-stellar guy, girl sleeps with less-than-stellar guy, and soon enough, girl is dating less-than-stellar guy. Repeat. You know the drill—you're living it.

This book will not reduce men's behaviors to a simple tagline. And it will not provide a neat and handy set of rules for you to follow. I'm giving you more credit than to assume you just need a rote list.

Instead, this book is designed to make you think about your actions and behaviors. That's right, even though it might be momentarily liberating to think, "Hey, it's not *my* fault it didn't work out, *he's just not that into me,*" it's just not that simple. Life doesn't let us off the hook so easily. And the idea that you are powerless to affect what a guy feels about you—that you might as well just be plucking the petals off of daisies ("he's into me, he's into me not") is part of the process of lowering your standards, abdicating responsibility for your actions, and accepting defeat.

There is no "right" or "wrong"; guys are not either "into you" or "not into you." The world is complex, and in the pages that follow, I'll outline a set of practical insights that will, I hope, help improve your love life. Based on my own experiences as a practicing sex therapist, current clinical studies, and a multitude of conversations I've had with men and women across the country, this book will help you become a little more honest with yourself and realize that you're the one who's not that into him. To achieve this, I've broken the book into three major parts, each addressing the ways in which women lower their standards. The goal of the book is to get you thinking and to pave the way for action, change, and the discovery of the love you want. To emphasize these points, each chapter concludes with two wrap-up sections. The first is called "Be Honest," and it functions as a two A.M. phone call from your best friend, the voice of reality. The second section, "Raise and Reach," provides some ideas on how to raise your standards and reach for the love you deserve.

When it comes to life, take the "you can't fire me because I quit" approach. He may not be that into you but, like the woman in black, it's worth remembering, "Guess what, guys? We're not that into you either!"

Stop lowering your standards, and start reaching for love! That may be easy for me to say and harder for you to do, but the first step is the realization that you're just not that into him. Action and reward will follow recognition.

Now, let's get going!

*part 1* SEX

*"Didn't your mother tell you that sex leads to things like dating?"*

—Frasier Crane to Roz
in an episode of *Frasier*

*S*EX HAPPENS. It's out there, everywhere, and you probably don't have to look that hard to find it. Thanks to the Internet, you can even look for sex (or socks, or both at the same time) from the comfort of your own home. Yes, women today have more sexual freedom than ever before, and a lot of you are taking advantage of this right. You are sensual, confident, open-minded, and prepared to go after what you want. And these instincts are not at odds with finding a man who will adore you.

And in the best-case scenario, you may be having all this sex with a guy you really like and who likes you. If so, I hope you're screwing like it's prom night and falling madly in love! But this is not always the situation. Most of you are single or in that chaotic limbo state of existence we call "dating." But still you find yourself horny, or lonely, or in between boyfriends.

So, what are your choices? Well, there's always Nick at Nite or your friendly neighborhood Rabbit but both of those get tiring, and after a while even the idea of a fresh set of Duracells starts to lose its luster. So, you call an ex or you go on a date and you meet a guy and soon enough you're sleeping with someone you know you are not really that into.

Men do this all the time, of course, because, well, they're men. But women can do it as well, and it can be exciting and perhaps even satisfying so long as you're being honest about your motivations and what you're getting (or, more likely, not getting) out of the bargain.

## The Horny Girl

> *"It sounds like a cliché, but I have needs as well. I get horny and I need to deal with it. And even when I know it's not the perfect situation, I sleep with guys I know I'm not into. Is it love? No. But at least it's another body."*
>
> —Karen, 33, advertising, Denver

Karen's situation is quite common. I hear stories like hers all the time in my work. Female desire, from a purely physiological point of view, often outpaces that of males.

Why? Well, as Hugh Hefner knows all too well, the female

body is built for sex. A woman is like a sleek, turbocharged Maserati compared to her male Yugo counterpart. And what is the engine that drives this pimped-out ride? The clitoris, which has no purpose other than sexual pleasure. It comes factory-built with twice as many nerve endings as the male penis (about eight thousand in total), an enviable anatomical reality that gives rise to multiple orgasms. (Viva la vulva!)

While guys are at their sexual best at about the time they can begin voting, women peak between their late twenties and early forties (among other proof points, women in their "sexual prime" report an increase in orgasms at these ages). While some of this can be attributed to hormonal changes, one major factor seems to be social conditioning. As women gain experience and self-confidence, they begin to feel more comfortable with themselves and their bodies. This in turn leads them to embrace erotic exploration as they discover their deeper sexual selves.

It's your world, ladies; we men just write books telling you how best to have sex in it.

## Booty Call Nation

*"I knew Mark from my old job, and while I thought he was cute, he was just not relationship material. We met for a drink one night, and one thing led to another. And because I knew him, it felt sort of secure, and he became a fuck buddy—nothing more. Men can do it, so why can't we?"*

—Cathy, 33, music industry executive, Los Angeles

Cathy's point is well taken. Not only does the current culture permit it, casual sex is encouraged these days. But when did the ball drop? While casual sex has been in existence since the beginning of time (remember Adam and Eve? the Roman orgies?), its genesis as an American cultural movement is often linked with the introduction of the birth control pill in the early 1960s, which helped catalyze the movement for sexual liberation. Women began embracing the power of their sexuality, and the feminist movement was as much about the right to proclaim pleasure as it was about equality elsewhere. No more would women accept sexless marriages and Victorian repression. (The vibrator was actually invented as a way of dealing with "female hysteria," which is what the Victorian medical establishment labeled female sexuality back then.)

The swinging sixties gave way to the hedonistic seventies, when Erica Jong introduced the "Me Generation" to the "zipless fuck," and sex without guilt became an accepted form of female behavior. Women, it seemed, were finally on top, getting it on with anonymous strangers on trains and in elevators. And where were modern men during all of this? On the sidelines, gleefully embracing this newfound "empowerment," of course.

Thanks to the seeds sown by the feminist movement, modern women were earning nearly as much as men by the 1990s, giving them unprecedented financial independence. Unburdened of the need to find a male provider, women were delaying marriage and enjoying dating as a form of sexual gratification. Enter *Sex and the City,* which exemplified a new form of empowerment: *a woman's ability to have sex like a man:* pleasure for the sake of pleasure.

And, like Carrie and her cronies, a lot of women today find themselves sleeping with guys they were never really that into to begin with. Again, this world of booty calls and one-night stands is a fine state of affairs if you're getting something out of the deal. Just be aware of what that something is. Sex is more than just an accessory in your wardrobe—a sheer Cosabella thong to be effortlessly slipped off before jumping into bed.

## The Lonely Heart/The Breakup Girl/ The In-Betweener

> *"I guess I was looking for something that would take my mind off things. I figured sex might help."*
>
> —Marie, 34, dental hygienist, Cleveland

Sometimes it is more than just a pure desire for sex that leads you to sleep with someone you are not that into. Sometimes you're just feeling lonely or in the throes of a recent breakup. Can sex help you get over someone else? Perhaps, though it can also make things worse. Can casual sex be a positive thing while you are waiting around for the love of your life to appear? Sure, as long as the casual sex is not keeping you from finding him or leaving you to confuse the in-betweener for the real thing.

Women sleep with men for a variety of reasons that have little to do with their libido. If you're aware of this, great. Go for it. Just be prepared to deal with the consequences that may arise.

But if you're looking to repair your self-esteem or exorcise the ghosts of boyfriends past through casual sex, you're probably setting yourself up for a disappointment.

## Giving Men What They Want

> *"A dating world where I can meet attractive, smart women who are sexually aware and who will sleep with me even though they don't really want a relationship? Let me check. Ya, I think I might be able to deal with that."*
>
> —Adam, 32, lawyer, Birmingham (Michigan)

While the conventional wisdom suggests otherwise, men are insecure and uncertain. Like women, we guys wonder whether you are into us, despite what certain books say. In *He's Just Not That into You,* the authors allude to the fact that if men can run the world, then they can call you first. Well, we're doing a fine job running things so far in this millennium, aren't we? And who are these men? I'm not quite sure myself. Most men I talk to are too preoccupied trying to understand the differences between Viagra, Levitra, and Cialis to run the world.

Women get nervous but men do too. That time we never called you—that might actually have been because we were confused—did you even want us to call you in the first place? Even though we're unsure, the pressure is on men to make the first move or advance the ball. Men are more than content to accept a world where there is sexual equality and where women can take charge—we just don't know how to handle it quite yet.

The potential downside to a scenario where women are as aggressive as men, and where casual sex is an accepted norm, is that it essentially gives men license to be, well, men. The biggest beneficiary of this female empowerment is the male. This is not to say that women should play by certain "rules" or withhold sex. That does not work, and it's silly gamesmanship. Or is it?

But on the flip side, you have to be aware that you might be contributing to the very situation that you often complain about: men who won't commit. We're not good on subtlety, especially when we're seeing a situation through testosterone-tinted glasses.

This is not to say that all men are incommunicative jerks or that the only thing we want is casual sex. We probably won't turn down a noncommittal roll in the hay, but that doesn't mean we see it as the pinnacle of existence—there is also baseball and beer, after all. Believe it or not, there are some guys who actually want to delay sex, especially with a woman they could potentially care about. And even when we're in situations that are casual, sometimes we're honest about that. It's not necessarily the case that a guy who says this is all he can handle is "not that into you." It's possible that, in fact, it's all he can handle, and if you both want to handle the same thing, i.e., casual sex (you go, girl!), perhaps it will be good for you too.

## THE "EVERYTHING-BUT GIRL"

Melissa is a thirty-five-year-old marketing executive living in Los Angeles. She is single but would like to be in a relationship, having been in the dating game for many years. She is independent and confident in her sexuality. Her experiences have led her to create her own set of rules. "If I like a guy, then I won't have sex with him right away," she says. "Blow jobs are fine but sex is something entirely different."

With her Clintonian parsing of the definition of sex, Melissa is an "everything-but girl" (EBG). That is, she will engage in *everything but* intercourse. This phenomenon seems to be widespread, as I have encountered EBGs from sea to shining sea.

The view is based on the belief that intercourse is somehow a more sacred, intimate act, that in opening oneself up, a woman makes herself more vulnerable than she does with other assorted (and, possibly, sordid) bedroom acts.

Is this view anachronistic or does intercourse have a potency that eclipses all other sex acts? There is no one answer. And while some might consider "everything but" a relatively random cutoff point, determining boundaries is an individual endeavor. We must all create our own definitions of sex (intern not included).

# The Flip Side: You Were Never That Into Him But the Sex Made You Think You Were

> *"I can sleep with a great-looking moron who can barely spell, and be aware of what I'm doing, but a day or so later,*

*I'm beginning to fantasize about picking out china patterns
with the guy. It's crazy but it happens every time I sleep
with someone."*

—Michelle, 28, public relations executive, New York

Michelle's situation raises a point that we'll cover in greater detail in the next chapter—that men and women have sex in very different ways. In many cases, even when a women is intellectually aware that she is not into the guy, somehow an emotional bond is formed. Some of this is due to the double standard that turns into remorse for "putting out" with a false belief that there was actually something more going on. Sometimes, the "liking him" feeling is really just an emotional justification for not liking him at all but still sleeping with him.

Some of it is chemical. When we have sex with someone new, there's a natural increase in certain hormones that tilt you toward caring about the person. Whether it was casual or not, sex causes the release of dopamine (the same chemical that's released in addicts). Dopamine causes excitement and focus. In addition, whether the sex led to orgasm or not, oxytocin is also emitted (no, that's not the stuff Rush Limbaugh was using). This is a very potent hormone that causes a woman to feel attached to the object she just slept with (even if he is a jerk who cannot spell "oxytocin"). The point is this: You can treat sex lightly but it doesn't reciprocate. Sex matters. There are biological and evolutionary forces at work every time you have sex, so just be honest with yourself about why you're doing it in the first place.

## Be Honest

It's a slippery slope (as it were), all this sexual empowerment. On the one hand, it's the apogee of the feminist revolution and the reclamation of female pleasure (and who doesn't love an apogee?). On the other hand, it may be the beginning of an imperceptible but very real slide downward, toward the land of lowered standards. Only you can really tell what effect your actions are having on your ability to have meaningful, gratifying sex when it counts. I'm just here to prompt the thought processes.

## Raise (Your Standards) and Reach (for Love)

- **You've earned it:** Sexual empowerment is a right and a privilege, so don't be afraid to use it. But use it wisely, and use it well.
- **Make sure it's a fair bargain:** If you are a woman and you go looking for casual sex, you're going to find it. And if you're having sex with a guy you know you're not that into, make sure you're getting something out of it.
- **Use the booty:** Guys are using you, so use back. Look at casual sex as a way to work on identifying your sexual wants and needs. Get comfortable communicating during sex—it gives you more power in the hookup and is great training for the relationship with the guy you're really into.

- **Check your head:** If you're being driven by something more than horniness, you may wind up liking the guy despite yourself. That's a trap, so ask yourself why you're having sex.
- **See the forest and the trees:** Sleep with enough guys you're not that into under the guise of being "in between" and then, suddenly, the between becomes the reality. Just be sure you're not missing out on what you really want by settling for what you think you need.
- **Sexpectations:** Are you sleeping with this guy because you want to and are filling some need or because he (or society) now "expects" you to do so? Empowerment gives you the right to have sex when you want to but you don't have to act in a sexually liberated manner if you don't feel like doing so.

## Casual Sex Glossary of Terms

**Booty call** *verb* or *noun* (1990s): A phone call, page, text message, instant message, or e-mail undertaken by one party to encourage the other to engage in casual sex, often occurring late at night. While either gender can instigate a booty call, it is most often engaged in by males under the influence of alcohol. In the noun form, the booty call is the one who receives the call and accepts the booty caller's invitation for a sexual liaison.

**Friend with benefits** *noun* (1990s): A FWB is a friend with whom you may occasionally hook up or have sex but without the deeper commitment of a relationship. The concept was de-scribed by Milan Kundera in *The Unbearable Lightness of Being* as an "erotic friendship." An FWB is more meaningful than an average booty call because often the participants were friends first and sex partners later.

**Fuck buddy** *noun* (1980s): A fuck buddy is a person with whom another has an ongoing, semiregular, no-strings-attached casual sex situation. Fuck buddies tend to be people with whom you have sex but no other semblance of a relationship. Fuck buddies often come in and out of each other's lives depending on whether one participant is engaged in other relationships.

**Hookup** *noun* (1990s): In the most general terms, a hookup is any sexual act with a person you are not dating or seriously commit-ted to. The hookup encompasses the booty call, the NSA, and the one-night stand. While the specifics of the scenario and the lan-guage used to describe it may change, the action upon which each of these definitions is built (i.e., the hookup) remains the same.

**No strings attached** *noun* (1970s): Hookups in which both partic-ipants are aware that there are no future expectations. NSA is a common abbreviation on ads posted on websites such as Craig's List, which features a section devoted to "Casual Encounters."

**One-night stand** *noun* (1970s): Hooking up with someone for one night of sex with no strings attached with the knowledge that you will never see the person again. A key element of the one-night stand is the conscious decision not to exchange personal information, such as telephone numbers or e-mail addresses.

**Walk of shame** *noun* (1980s): The post-booty-call walk home, most often undertaken in the same clothing worn the evening before. While the term often refers to a walk across a college campus, it is also a common occurrence in urban areas. If, for example, you see a woman in heels and a dress getting into a cab on a Saturday morning while you are fetching coffee, she is likely engaged in a walk (or cab ride) of shame.

**Zipless fuck** *noun* (1973): A phrase coined by Erica Jong in *Fear of Flying*. As described in the book, it refers to a sexual encounter between strangers that has the swift compression of a dream and is free of all remorse and guilt. It is pure, free of power games and ulterior motives.

## 2. YOU'RE NOT THAT INTO HIM EITHER, BUT YOU THOUGHT YOU COULD HAVE SEX LIKE A MAN

*"Did the last four and a half hours mean nothing to you?"*

—Charlotte of *Sex and the City*, shouting at a guy she just hooked up with

It's a question for the ages: If men are capable of having sex without any meaning or attachment, why can't women? You broke the glass ceiling, you have your own basketball league, and you pretty much run the world (or, you ought to). And whether guys understand them or not, it's clear that you women have the tools (with or without the Rabbit) to be as sexual as men. But having orgasms is just one aspect of sex. There's also that pesky emotional component that women seem to have the tools for too, and in greater measure, I might add.

Now, some of you are out there are having casual sex with guys you're not into because you think you can and *should* have sex like men. Maybe you can. But, more than likely, you've tried to behave this way, only to discover that at the end of the day (or night), something just isn't quite right.

Perhaps the sex you're having is *not that great*. Or perhaps you find yourself getting emotionally involved even when you've convinced yourself (and the guy you're with) that it's meant to be light and casual. And, more than likely, you wind up asking yourself why. What am I doing wrong? How can I start having good sex with someone I actually like? Is that really so much to ask for?

Now, I'm not telling you that you can't have sex like a man but think about this: If women were really disposed to have sex like men, wouldn't women be greater consumers of porn and prostitution? It's not as if women do not have socioeconomic bargaining chips. No doubt about it, if the demand were there, the product would be as well.

*Playgirl*'s efforts to launch an adult-oriented network aimed at women notwithstanding, when was the last time you avoided your job to surf the Internet to look at naked men? That guy you're sleeping with? He probably gets up from *having sex with you* to browse online for porn.

Women and men are not from different planets, despite all allegations to the contrary, but they do experience sex in galactically different ways. And even if that may seem obvious, the reasons behind these differences may shed some new light on some very old and ongoing issues.

## Difference One: Your Ever-Elusive Orgasm

*"Nature is cruel. Sure, I'm more sexually aware than ever.*
*But competing with that awareness is my desire to be in a*
*committed relationship. For a while I thought that lots of*
*sex with guys that I don't care that much about might be*
*okay, but even the sex was not so great. I'm kind of stuck*
*between a rock and a hard, um, vibrator."*

—Amanda, 32, lawyer, Chicago

As any man who has spent time in the trenches will tell you, the female orgasm is an elusive thing. Like Bigfoot and quality television, we know it's out there; we just don't actually come into contact with the real thing all that often. While the clitoris is clearly built for bliss, understanding female sexuality is as complicated as Euclidean geometry, and the female orgasm is the final exam. Most men fail miserably (we're not graded on a curve), though it's not entirely our fault, especially if you're having sex with a guy you're really not that into in the first place.

Why is it so hard for women to achieve orgasm when all a guy needs is a glimpse at the lingerie section of a Sears catalog? Some evolutionary anthropologists conjecture that the physiological difficulty works like a built-in monogamy device. Here's the logic: Because the female orgasm is so tricky to achieve, its mastery requires dedication and patience, an extended "getting to you know" process (this explains why women have to "concentrate" to orgasm). This encourages a woman to seek relationships with one partner, a guy who can spend the energy and time to familiarize himself with her sexuality. As with getting to

Carnegie Hall, perfection requires practice, practice, practice (though the N train will take you right there as well).

This orgasm issue is borne out by clinical studies. From a purely orgasmic point of view, women in relationships fare far better than single women. As cited by Jonathan Margolis in his book *O: The Intimate History of the Orgasm,* a 1977 survey by *Redbook* magazine of 100,000 respondents revealed that women who were more sexually adventurous and experimental had fewer orgasms than women who, if they had sex at all before marriage (many in the survey had not), had it with men they loved and subsequently married. Among the respondents who had had a series of one-night stands, 77 percent said they *never* reached orgasm during such sessions. Again, we see that the pleasure-producing properties of the magical clitoris are better served by one good lover than by many mediocre ones. And while this Carter-era survey may seem dated, these findings are borne out today in sex therapy.

Now, here's a curveball for you: As it turns out, there are components to sex that outweigh even the much-sought-after orgasm.

## Difference Two: Your Emotional Quotient

> *"Free, we say, yet the truth is they get erections when they're with a woman they don't give a damn about but we don't have an orgasm unless we love him. What's free about that?"*
>
> —Doris Lessing, *The Golden Notebook*

Though it was written in the early 1960s, Lessing's complaint describes a dilemma that many women still face in the new millennium: You may be free to pursue sex like men but the deeper pleasures require some level of emotional attachment. The question is this: Do women need at least some sense of connection in order to achieve orgasm? One way to answer this question may be to look at what happens when there is a lack of emotional rapport.

Unlike corporate executives and politicians, your orgasms never lie. They tell you the truth about a sexual encounter, whether you want to know it or not. In clinical terms, the female orgasm releases a burst of oxytocin, also known as the cuddle hormone. It's what makes you feel warm and fuzzy and what facilitates a sense of attachment. But if there's nothing to attach to, if there's no deeper emotional content or meaningfulness, orgasm becomes a regretful reminder of the hollowness of the sex that preceded it. This is called *post-orgasm regret,* and it typically manifests itself in the form of sadness or anger. If you've ever felt a pang of sorrow following a sexually gratifying (i.e., orgasmic) hookup, it's most likely post-orgasmic regret (though his low-thread-count sheets may also be a contributing factor).

But what if you're not having orgasms to begin with? Well, you may be experiencing *post-faking regret*—regretting that you helped him get off while you faked it. Of course, there is no scientific evidence to back that up. Orgasm or not, be aware that for women, sex results in your body inching toward some emotional connection, even as your brain is saying, "What the hell am I doing in bed with this balding, out-of-shape accountant?"

## IS THERE AN EVOLUTIONARY IMPERATIVE?

Much is made of the notion that men and women are guided by different and, in many ways, competing evolutionary imperatives. Men, so the theory goes, are driven to spread their seed to as many willing recipients as possible and are thus biologically inclined to be promiscuous (and, apparently, to recline in large chairs). Women, ostensibly seeking to further the race, search for a single strong provider. Sex, under the female scenario, is more a means to an end.

In *O: The Intimate History of the Orgasm,* Jonathan Margolis expands on this idea. "It would seem that for women across cultures, during an individual act of sex, the journey—from wooing to scene setting to foreplay—is all-important, while the consummatory end is very much a secondary goal," he writes. "This apparent reality has contributed to the common—and possibly correct—view of women as 'traders,' who exchange sexual favors for security rather than for sex."

So even with the safety of contraception and the knowledge that they can pursue pleasure purely for the sake of pleasure, there is some evolutionary fail-safe mechanism in place that prevents women from having sex like men.

In this day of hyperspeed connections, both online and into bed, what are your options? If other women are hooking up in order to get male attention, for the moment or the long haul, do you really have any choice? Yes, of course you do. For as much as we are creatures of our own biological imperatives, we humans are also equipped with the ability to make conscious choices and to fight these more primordial urges. You don't need to trade to find the love you're looking for but you do need to take stock of yourself, your standards, and how your actions are impacting those things.

## Difference Three: You're Not AATO
## (All About The Orgasm)

*"The orgasm is the cherry on the sundae—tasty, but all
parts are delicious."*

—Leslie, 28, makeup artist, Cleveland

I've been giving the orgasm a lot of airtime, so it may seem odd
for me to suggest that there are other facets of the sexual experience that might be more important. One question I often ask
women is this: If you don't orgasm, is the sex still enjoyable? Almost all say yes, citing intimacy and affection as their principal
reasons for liking sex. Now, men can, and do, enjoy affection but
for them the orgasm and the sex are virtually one and the same
(this has roots in biology, as they seek to spread their seed). Men
are goal-oriented, whereas women enjoy all the various parts of
the experience, even if they don't "get off" per se.

When asked to describe the best part of sex, many women
cite the first moment of penetration, not the orgasm. When
asked why, almost all mention the sense of connectedness this act
brings with it. This is especially ironic when you consider that
almost all of the sensitive nerve endings that contribute to the female orgasm are located on the surface of the vulva and require
external stimulation, rather than penetration, in order to spark
sexual response.

In fact, most sexual positions, especially the beloved mission-
ary (the most popular in the world, according to anthropologists), miss the clitoris altogether. But whether it's a result of
cultural or emotional factors, or simply the symbolic procreative

possibilities that are attendant to the act, intercourse seems to carry emotional pleasures for women that outweigh the physiological component of sexual response. This is not true of men. Rare is the man who can enjoy sex without orgasm or even separate the two (unless he's one of these Tantric types, and then you'll have to deal with his penchant for sarongs and chanting).

I'm not suggesting that you should reorient yourself away from orgasm, but I also believe that we live in an age of "regretful orgasms." I want your orgasms to be blissful and gratifying. Sure you can have sex like a man, but you shouldn't do so at the expense of having sex like a woman.

## Difference Four: You May Need Something More

> *"I've definitely slept with guys who I knew I would never get involved with. But to do so I had to shut off my emotions, and that made me a cold person. And in doing so, I short-circuited my ability to really enjoy it."*
>
> —Christine, 28, financial services vice president,
> San Francisco

With the knowledge that a casual sex encounter is less likely to bring the reward of an orgasm or any deeper emotional benefits, what do you get out of it? And are the costs of hooking up greater than the benefits? Do the booty-call math and determine for yourself.

For some women, a casual hookup can be a place where they "practice" for the real thing. Unburdened by any concern over whether the guy will like them in the future, such women use hookups as a preseason warm-up. Others claim that the anonymity allows them to be more wild and carefree than they normally would be.

One of the potential costs of a casual hookup, however, is that it can be deceiving. What you may view as casual and meaningless can give rise to a sense of attachment, placing you on the roller coaster of emotional involvement. We humans don't require all that much to begin to believe that another person cares about us or finds us special. Even women who go into a situation fully aware that there is no commitment, that it's just "no-strings-attached" sex, may come out on the other side with genuine feelings for the guy.

Some women (patients, friends, the woman at my dry cleaner) get pissed off at me when I suggest that sex and emotions are more inextricably linked in women than in men but I mean this as a compliment to female sexuality. As a man and a sex therapist, I can assure you that men ultimately want more than hollow orgasms too, but they have to work harder at it. You can teach yourself to have sex like a man but that doesn't mean that men, deep down, wouldn't rather learn to have sex like a woman.

And even if you don't pay an emotional cost, there may, unfortunately, be a societal toll. For as liberated as the world may be, there is still a double standard that equates hypersexuality among women with being slutty—the strut of shame, new millennium style. Is this an old-fashioned and ignorant judgment? Sure, but it still exists. According to a recent survey of three thousand women, 25 percent agreed they could have one-night stands without becoming even somewhat attached, but 80 percent of such women regretted their conduct, which sometimes made them "feel like sluts."

The issue is really how you deal with this behavior, and how much you care what other people think. If you're dating a guy and you think you may like him, such behavior may turn him off. As we will discuss later, the pursuit and achievement of sex has unexpected consequences in the way it functions in the male brain. The more he works for it, the more he is likely to savor it, and the more likely that process of pursuit will fuel romantic love.

Does this mean you should play hard to get? Not at all, especially if you're just in it for the sex. But don't beat yourself up for being "easy" or blame him for thinking the same—the whole point of casual sex is to make it easy. But that doesn't mean there isn't some social stigma attached to it, whether it's backward or not. It's why the term "easy" is often used interchangeably with more derogatory terms. Are you being easy when you have casual sex? Of course you are, but why would you want it to be hard? Unless, of course, you end up feeling either remorseful or sad that it doesn't turn into something more.

## Be Honest

Yes, you can have sex like a man. Sort of. Should you? Well, that's up to you. There are some physical and emotional differences between the sexes. And casual sex often looks better on the surface than it actually turns out to be in real life. As much as you want to enjoy sexual empowerment and pursue pleasure, you just might not be capable of "dumbing down" sex. Hooking up can be a form of settling. It's like getting junk food on the run when you're really hungry. For the moment, it's satisfying, but it generally leaves you promising yourself "never again."

## Raise (Your Standards) and Reach (for Love)

- **It's your call:** You can have sex like a man but just know that the more casual the situation, the less likely it is you'll achieve orgasm or any emotional state of happiness.
- **Trust what sex tells you:** If you feel angry or regretful after a sexual encounter, listen to it. Conversely, if you feel a sense of warmth, you might be on to something.
- **The means or the end?** Can you compartmentalize between the pleasures of sex and its emotional qualities? If you're having casual sex as a means to an end (the pleasure of a flesh-on-flesh orgasm), navigating the "means" may be trickier than expected.
- **Define yourself:** Some sex acts carry more weight than others for a whole variety of reasons—rational and irrational. Even if something seems irrational, trust your instincts.
- **Don't internalize:** Social judgments and your own moral compass may make you feel like what you're doing is wrong. If so, change your behavior, but don't internalize the judgments of others.

## 3. YOU'RE NOT THAT INTO HIM EITHER, BUT THAT DIDN'T STOP HIM FROM HAVING SEX LIKE A MAN

*"Women need a reason for having sex, men just need a place."*

—*City Slickers*

*A*s we discussed in the last chapter, a lot of women are out there trying to have sex like men. But what does "having sex like a man" even mean? In lieu of finding yourself in yet another remake of *Freaky Friday* and waking up with a penis, you'll never *really* know what it's like. But that's okay because I'm going to walk you through it.

Do men really have sex in such different ways than women? If so, are the differences societal or biological? And what is it about men that makes them able to derive pleasure from situations in which they are emotionally removed?

For one potential answer, let's turn to nature and explore why "animal attraction" is the rule rather than the exception (if this were biology class, we'd be showing a filmstrip right now, so don't fall asleep!).

## Of Rats and Men

> *"Of course the idea of love and happiness and all that stuff is appealing. But what does that have to do with getting laid?"*
>
> —Steven, 33, real estate broker, Atlanta

To be honest, the guy you slept with (yes, that one, with the heavy Drakar Noir habit) didn't just have sex like a man, he had sex like a rat. What do I mean by this? Well, like most mammals, rats are not monogamous. Their main concern is the act of sex, not the partner they are having sex with. Sounds familiar, I'm sure. In this analogy, rats stand in contrast to the prairie vole, a cute little critter that has the notable distinction of being among the 3 percent of all mammals that mate for life. (That's right, 97 percent of mammals don't, including most of the men you are likely to bring home from a bar at two A.M.)

Unlike rats, voles are selective. Yep, they actually care about who they sleep with because the sex is part of an overall mating process. They're in it for the long haul. Voles aren't into hooking up, but once they've chosen a mate, they copulate like mad (over fifty times in two days) and then set about the business of bonding for life: nesting, mating, protecting, and nurturing. In voles, the sex seals the deal; in rats it's just a means to an end: more sex.

Now, while it might be tempting to suggest that men are rats and women are voles, in my experience, it's not as cut and dry as all that (there's a little bit of rat in all you women, and most men have an inner vole, somewhere deep, *deep* inside).

As it turns out, rats and voles do have a few things in common. Both produce a chemical in the brain called dopamine. Ogden Nash wrote that "candy is dandy, but liquor is quicker." Well, dopamine leaves both in the dust. Dopamine is considered a natural amphetamine, and it plays a key role in both sexual arousal and goal attainment. Dopamine gets us hooked on sex; it's part of the cocktail of sex chemicals that intoxicate us during the act. But give dopamine a chance and it performs a feat of alchemy: It transforms the raw heat of testosterone into romantic love. When sex is denied, it triggers the reward centers in the male brain—he wants it all the more, and dopamine is what fuels the chase.

Dopamine is the stuff of "absence makes the heart grow fonder." But when it's triggered during casual sex, it doesn't get the chance to strut its stuff. In rats, the dopamine fuels the pursuit of the next orgasm, which is usually just around the corner. But it is the presence of two other hormones—vasopressin (in men) and oxytocin (in women)—that lead us to connect our dopamine-triggered emotions to a single person, thereby inspiring monogamy. As we mentioned in the last chapter, oxytocin is the hormone that is responsible for post-orgasm regret. When you are with someone you care about, oxytocin gives you the bliss of feeling complete when he holds you in his arms. In men, vasopressin helps him feel protective and loving (and, down the line, paternal). Think of these hormones as a beer chaser to the dopamine shot—they take the edge off but also make the hunt worthwhile.

When you have sex for sex's sake with someone you're not really that into, you're tapping into your inner rat instead of seeking out the inner vole in your ideal rattish mate. It's important to note, from a physiological standpoint, that the same chemicals that inspire him to fuck like a rat can also enlighten him to make love like a vole.

Sex is powerful stuff and one of the downsides of having it casually is that it devalues a core component of the courtship process: what I tend to call the dance or, for you alpha voles out there, the hunt. Not to say you can't have casual sex, fall in love, and live happily ever after, but it's less likely, and certainly more of a challenge, when you consider how we're wired. The truth is that nature rigged our wiring before contraception and the sexual revolution overhauled the system.

So what does that mean? Basically that nature is ultimately more concerned with ensuring the propagation of future generations than with providing a good lay for you.

## The Trigger-Happy Male

> "There are some days when I literally cannot leave my office to get lunch, for fear that my head will explode at the sheer amount of female beauty on the streets of this city. It's like a sea of sex."
>
> —Mark, 35, investment banker, New York

How often do you think about sex over the course of a day? Figure it out, now add one, and then multiply that number by a hundred—that's probably the minimum number of times a man thinks about it. Why add one? Because some women don't think about sex at all during the day, at least not in a graphic manner.

That doesn't mean that women don't think about sex—it's actually much to the contrary. It's just that women don't think about it in the same way as men. Men respond heavily to external triggers such as porn, billboards, and a woman walking by in a miniskirt. They're driven so crazy by external triggers that sometimes all they can do is think about sex. And trust me, it's no picnic.

Women think about sex more often when it's internally triggered—by thoughts of a guy they like, or a past boyfriend, or sometimes just a situation that's special. Men almost always fantasize and masturbate to thoughts of body parts—they're intuitive objectifiers, whereas women are more situationally driven; it's part of the reason that the new generation of female-centric porn focuses more heavily on plot and story instead of the popular "money shots" found in traditional male-focused adult films.

That said, when a guy puts his imagination to work and masturbates to the internal triggers, it's very often to a woman he cares about or has once cared about. He may be trigger-happy for you but is it because you're a hot piece of ass, or something more special, and specific?

## Love at First Erection?

*"Truth is, guys can size up a woman pretty quickly. There are really three buckets: women with relationship potential, women you're just interested in having sex with, and women you wouldn't touch with a ten-foot pole. But that's*

*the problem with poles: You won't touch her with a ten-*
*foot one but that doesn't mean you won't touch her with a*
*six-inch one."*

—Jack, 32, lawyer, Cleveland

From Romeo and Juliet to Dawson and Joey on *Dawson's Creek,* we're drawn to the romantic idea of love at first sight. But is love at first sight a male way of seeing things? Are men more likely to experience the phenomenon than women? In my surveys of happily married couples, when asked, "At what point in your relationship did you know for sure that you wanted to spend the rest of your lives with each other," invariably the men are much more likely to have had definitive feelings at the outset, whereas most women said they needed time to make up their minds. (Speaking for myself, I was getting hooked on my wife after the second date but it took her significantly longer to decide that I was the one.)

According to noted anthropologist Helen Fisher, author of the remarkable book *Why We Love,* scientists have observed that when falling in love, there is greater activity in the parts of the male brain associated with visual processing than there is in the corresponding parts of the female brain, as well as greater activity in the parts of the brain associated with sexual arousal. "When the time is right and a man *sees* an attractive woman, he is anatomically equipped to rapidly associate attractive *visual* features with feelings of romantic passion. What an effective courtship device." This is likely what makes him bring you flowers.

Actually, this visualization propensity works in the reverse as well, which is why men's ability to select such a wide range of bedmates is often criticized. Men experience a phenomenon known as "pre-orgasm anticipation." This sensation is so potent that it can actually influence the male brain to develop this association seemingly out of thin air. Because of this, as our opportunities for casual sex in a given situation dwindle, our ability to justify a wider array of options increases.

Translation: We'll take any women left standing. Some guys like to call it "beer goggles," but alcohol or not, men will lower their standards to levels women can't begin to fathom—hence the aging, toothless prostitute who still manages to amass a tidy profit. We may feel like getting the hell out of Dodge the moment the deed is done but damned if we don't work hard to get there to begin with.

Now, I'm going to tell you something you probably already know: Men are run by their erections. But what you really need to know is which sort of erection is doing his thinking. Well, it all depends, because there are three types.

The first type, produced by erotic stimuli, is considered a **psychogenic erection**, or what I like to think of as a "brain erection." Men also experience **reflex erections** as a result of direct genital stimulation, which is what I like to think of as a "body erection." And finally, men also experience **nocturnal erections**, which occur spontaneously during REM cycles, which is why guys are generally the first to wake up wanting morning sex.

In terms of psychogenic erections, experiments have shown that audio and visual stimuli are pivotal in stimulating an erection, which is why guys respond so easily to porn. Women respond to psychogenic material as well but there need to be other components, which is where emotional differences between the sexes come into play.

Reflex erections are caused by the stimulation of local nerve impulses originating in the genital area. Manual or oral stimulation will stimulate nerve fibers in the penis, activating a reflex circuit that sets in motion a series of events that increase blood flow into the penis and create an erection. This is why men respond so much more quickly to physical stimulation, and why physical stimulation alone can be used to, um, get the balls rolling. This also explains why female prostitutes can receive all sorts of physical stimulation (and give it as well) without being the least bit turned on. Unlike men, women don't respond as simply to these external stimuli.

## Mr. Compartmental

*"My last boyfriend claimed to really love me but that didn't stop him from cheating on me with a stripper. He apologized and made a lot of excuses about it just being sex, but when I'm in love, I don't want to have sex with anybody else."*

—Jane, 30, student, Berkeley

As we're discovering, there are fundamental differences between men and women when it comes to sex, and part of this is rooted in the way desire and arousal are linked in men.

To illustrate this point, we turn now to our bigwig pharmaceutical friends. Pfizer was so "pumped up" about the success of Viagra on men that they couldn't wait to develop a little blue pill for women. But after clinical tests on thousands of women—conducted just as they had been on men, with a pill and some porn—they ultimately abandoned the effort completely.

Why? While Viagra had the same physiological effects on women as it did on men (it stimulated blood flow to the genitals), it did not create a concurrent desire for sex. The Viagra left women feeling tingly in their pelvises, but not much else.

This led Pfizer and others to conclude that men are both genitally and visually focused when it comes to sexual desire—give a guy a hard-on and he wants to use it—and that desire is a much trickier matter in women. If you want to understand what makes women tick sexually you have to get inside their heads. For men, desire and arousal are virtually one in the same but for women, desire usually requires components that don't necessarily need to be present for men: intimacy, affection, trust, humor, respect, and a sense of security. Men appreciate those things too, but we don't necessarily require them to get turned on and have sex.

This difference in how men experience desire explains why we're able to compartmentalize sex and love. It also explains why we are the main purveyors of porn and prostitutes. All it takes is an external trigger to stimulate desire, which in turn stimulates arousal. Or vice versa: All it takes is a little physical arousal to stimulate desire. In men, it's a simple self-feeding cycle. This is not so in women. Desire leads to arousal for women, but arousal doesn't always lead to desire.

## The Flip Side: Men Have Feelings Too

Though it's my contention that men are more "ratlike" than women, it's worth remembering that there are at least two sides to male sexuality. On the one hand, men are more able to compartmentalize love and sex, which allows them to have sex without emotion. But that does not mean they don't want the emotion. As a sex therapist, I meet with a lot of guys who have cheated, or are thinking about it, and many are searching for an emotional connection that they're no longer getting at home. My experiences have been supported by conversations with other sex therapists: Men are ultimately looking for more than just a quick lay, which explains why casual sex often isn't enough, in and of itself, to trigger romantic love, or why when sex becomes routine and mechanical in a long-term relationship it also becomes unfulfilling. Men may be more easily aroused but that does not make them any less fundamentally interested in romantic or emotionally based love.

In addition, it explains another difference between men and women when it comes to sex: When a man is with someone he loves, he views sex as the ultimate emotional expression. Sex is a way of expressing his emotions, and many women just don't get this because they're so adept at expressing their emotions in other ways. In men, making love and expressing love are one and the same, which is why some men often wait to have sex, or avoid intimate acts like cunnilingus. What he does, or doesn't do, is sometimes an expression of how he feels.

## Be Honest

There are rats and there are voles, and maybe when you have casual sex you're a vole in rat's clothing.

When you consider our biological wiring, some of the old

adages, like playing hard to get, might make sense. But not because you're playing a game—it's just that sex is relative. There are no absolutes: Sex can be as frivolous or intimate as you make it. Problem is, sometimes for one partner (generally the one who shaves more often), it's akin to masturbation, while for the other it spells the beginning of an emotional connection. Even when women and men start out at ground level in a sexual encounter, something happens differently. Call it physiology but more often than not, men tend to turn into rats, while women turn into voles.

## Raise (Your Standards) and Reach (for Love)

*Is he a rat or a vole?*

- **Booty caller or man with a plan?** Voles have no shortage of sex drive (they sometimes have sex more than fifty times in a couple of days) but they have a selection process. They want sex to be with someone they can mate with for life. Not so the rats. Voles plan ahead.
- **Getting to know you:** If he's a vole, not only is he going to want sex as part of a broader relationship, he'll also want to get to know you as a person beyond the sex, and as important, he'll want you to get to know him.
- **Seeing eye to eye:** In my experience, rats have no problem with sex. The voles are the ones who have the issues because they attach significance and intimacy to certain acts (intercourse, giving oral sex) and may want to delay these acts if they want to realize the full significance.

Think of it this way—he might be avoiding certain acts because he doesn't associate you with that level of intimacy.

- **How giving and affectionate is he during the act?** Does he kiss you? Does he do so tenderly? Guys understand the difference between fucking and making love, and they are going to be more intimate, more gentle, and more tender with someone they're serious about.

- **A rat in vole's clothing:** Talk is cheap for a lot of guys, and there are definitely those who understand how easy it is to compliment, hype, and even say "I love you." So, when you think back over your encounters, put the sound on mute and play over his actions. Rats talk to have sex, voles communicate.

- **Remember post-orgasm regret?** Guys experience it too, in the form of a sense of entrapment and desire to flee. Men will say or do pretty much anything to get to orgasm but within moments of the event, it's possible for them to experience a rat version of orgasm regret. If he's fidgety, like a trapped animal, talking about all the work he has to do and checking his e-mail on his BlackBerry, he very well may be willing to chew his arm off to escape your trap.

4. MULTIPLE CHOICES, VOLUME 1

*K*aren is a thirty-three-year-old marketing executive. She lives in Chicago, Illinois, where she has been since graduating from the University of Virginia in 1993. She works for a small fashion company, and she loves what she does. Her job takes her to New York City and Europe at least once a season. She is confident, self-assured, and generally content with her life. She does not feel it necessary to have a man for financial or emotional support. That said, she is reflective enough to know that she does want to get married and have children. Not in the next week but at some point in the future.

Tonight, however, Karen faces some options. It is

Friday, and she's had a long week at work. She is stressed out and, frankly, feeling a little bit randy. To make matters worse, her last serious boyfriend (Steve, a lawyer, whom she dated for two years) just got engaged, and she found out via a mass e-mail that a former mutual friend sent out. This was the perfect capper to a tough week.

For the purposes of this exercise, you control Karen's fate for the evening. In this two-dimensional simulation, you choose the outcome of her life (or, at least, her Friday night).

Karen has the following options. She can:

**a)** Stay at home with a nice bottle of wine, order in Japanese food, do some laundry, surf a few Internet dating sites, and then masturbate before going to bed at a reasonable hour.

**b)** Meet some girlfriends at a bar to drink, talk, survey the crowds, and generally carouse in a manner that is tasteful but leaves open the possibility for fun.

**c)** Reply to an e-mail that Greg, a fuck buddy, wrote earlier in the week, asking what she was doing on Friday evening, knowing full well that he is available and ready, and not half bad in the sack.

**d)** Write a long-winded letter of complaint to the author of this book, suggesting that his quiz is predicated on generalities and is mildly patronizing to women.

Please take out your number two pencil and, using the space provided below, select the best answer from the choices listed above. Then write why you believe this to be the best option in twenty words or less.

When you are done, please put your pencil down and turn the page for the answer key. You have five minutes to complete this test.

---

**PLEASE WORK IN THIS BOX**

---

—DO NOT TURN PAGE UNTIL YOU HAVE
COMPLETED THIS TEST—

*Answer Key:*

Which answer did you choose? Hmm. If you chose any one answer, you fell for our clever (and possibly annoying) trap. The correct answer is all of the above. On any given Friday evening, Karen (or you, for that matter) could have chosen any one of the options (there is even the possibility that more than one option could occur over the course of a night), depending on how she felt. There is no single "correct" answer. There are only choices.

If this were a book predicated on laying out "rules" or a simplistic "program" (i.e., if I wanted to insult your intelligence), I might be telling you that one choice was "correct," and that there was a prescribed set of behaviors you could follow to get the guy and find love.

But you know that's not how the world works, and I know you know that.

Still, there is some value (even if it's just entertainment) in looking at how each of the various choices might have played out. . . .

To that end, I thus present to you: "Karen's Friday Night, Parts 1–3"

## Choice A: The Stay-at-Homer

Staying home on a Friday night. For married people, it's called "life." For single people, it's a luxury. More often than you'd care to recall, your Friday nights have been spent seated across from a mediocre date or in yet another bitching session with the girls. Staying home and doing nothing may seem like an attractive choice when compared to these options. Staying at home and doing nothing can be a healthy option when you are tired of the world and want to regroup. You're not an amateur; you don't need to go out just to say you went out.

So, tonight, after finally getting off of a long conference call, Karen makes a quick trip to the gym and then retires to her sofa and uncorks a bottle of Geyser Creek Pinot Noir (1998), given to her by an in-the-meantimer who happened to have halfway decent taste in wine (and thus lasted three dates past his vintage).

She had a week's worth of unopened mail to tend to, laundry in desperate need of washing, and an unwatched DVD from Netflix sitting on her coffee table. This was more than enough to occupy her for the evening. And besides, it would allow her to get up early tomorrow and tackle the weekend with a clear, hangover-free head. Yes, she'd finally visit that Monet exhibit, grab lunch with a friend, and even replace her old shower curtain.

She dons her favorite sweats, puts up her hair, and organizes her night. She puts her darks in the washing machine, then orders dinner, and has that load ready for the dryer once the sushi arrives. In the meantime, she'll sort her mail (mostly bills and, of course, two engagement party invites). Anything, really, to occupy her mind so that she's less aware she's home, alone.

The food arrives, just as the washer finishes its final spin cycle. The night was going according to plan. But about halfway into the bottle of wine, having finished with her miso soup and sushi, she starts to feel a mild pang of curiosity. And though she had told herself she was going to take a break from online dating, her laptop beckoned, as it often did. She heeds the call.

When she logs onto Match.com she finds six new notes from prospective suitors. *"I'm desired,"* the unopened messages seem to say. And for a moment she feels flush with the hope of romantic possibility. While she deletes four of the notes immediately (three had no pictures and one was from a married man looking for "fun"), the two that remain have potential, or so it seems. She decides not to reply that night (what would these guys think if they knew she had been home on a Friday, answering her e-mails), but spends another forty minutes browsing through the profiles. As often happens, she sees men she'd been out with before (some of whom, while less than stellar, never called her for a second date). A small pond, and one filled by the same fish.

Slightly ruffled, but still giddy that she has seen a few new options, she logs off and retires to her bedroom and the comfort of her oft-used vibrator (not the Rabbit, which her friends raved about, but a more mundane Dolphin that, along with her fingers, does the trick better than most of the men she's dated recently). Another Friday night in the big city comes to a close with a self-induced bang. Folding her laundry will wait until tomorrow.

## Choice B: The Girl's Night Out

[Disclaimer: If this scenario seems clichéd, it's probably because all the best situations involving single urban women have already been used by *Sex and the City*.

After a hard week of making the world safe for cashmere ponchos, Karen feels she deserves a night out with her closest girlfriends (or, at least, those among her friends who are not married or otherwise disengaged from bar nights). Her friend Stephanie, the wild one of the group, is on the list for a party at

Sapphire, a new velvet-roped and doorman club in Wicker Park (Chicago's answer to Greenwich Village). Being on the list means they do not have to wait in an endless line or pay the ridiculous cover charge, but it will not protect them from the men on the prowl inside. But Karen's not complaining. If the night's plans had been up to her, they'd have gone to McKinnon's, a local pub near her apartment with a fireplace and a decibel level that actually allows a group of friends to do more than yell, *"What??"* to one another over the din of techno music. But Stephanie is leading the charge, and Karen plays the dutiful companion, donning her Seven jeans and her pointy Prada pumps, and heads out into the promise of yet another Friday night.

Sapphire. Even the name screams "trendy beyond any reason to visit in the first place." But there they are, Karen and five of her closest friends (two of the women were college roommates and the other three are industry friends). They are all single (Stephanie had been married once, and two others had recently left long-term live-in situations), and smart enough to know that the only men inside the club are guys they'd never really be that into (but who would, nonetheless, buy them $15 drinks). So why are they there? Well, the heart always holds out hope that the mind knows may not likely be met. But that hope is what gets us out on a Friday night, isn't it? It's always *possible* that the love of our lives is inside the same miserable club we are walking into, tucked away in a corner, waiting for us to make an entrance.

The evening progresses, and trays of expensive, fruit-based drinks are ordered (and, subsequently, spilled). Much laughter is had. Dancing follows, and soon the girls are invited to the VIP room by a group of commodities traders celebrating a big week at the exchange (coffee futures, my friend, coffee futures). The men are harmless—good-time guys, a little heavy on the white bread, but nice enough to share a bottle of champagne with. Karen has a hard time telling them apart as they essentially look like copies of one another (and every other guy with short hair, a business degree, and the ability to walk into Banana Republic) but she's up for the challenge.

And then a funny thing happens. As the night wears on, and the mini-party progresses, Karen and one of the traders begin to talk. Sweet James (as he calls himself) is not the best looking of the bunch but he is very complimentary, and the attention makes Karen feel special. He was, as his self-proclaimed title suggests, very sweet. Basking in this warm glow, Karen starts to loosen up (the Ketel One and Red Bulls they are downing help as well), so much so that she allows James to feel her out as they dance to that "dirty" Christina Aguilera remix. She is getting sloppy, yes, but who would possibly recognize her amid the strobe lights and artificial fog? Moreover, she is a sexually liberated woman, and she has the right to do as she pleases. Leaving the dance floor, she and James find a quiet banquette and proceed to get freaky, two urban professionals letting their hair down after a long week. The man she is mashing in the corner is not the man she will marry but Karen is willing to put up with the Mr. Wrongs until Mr. Right comes along.

## CUT TO:
## INTERIOR: KAREN'S OFFICE, FIVE DAYS LATER

Karen does not go home with Sweet James (even after much deliberation). Still, she finds herself hoping to hear from him. When he put her in a cab at the end of the night, they exchanged business cards, and he said he'd "shoot her an e-mail during the week." He mentioned the possibility of getting a drink, which she knew meant he was interested in sex, not dating. This week is now halfway over, and she's not heard from him. So here she is, seated in her office, hitting the SEND/REPLY button on her e-mail program, willing his note to appear in her in-box. Not that she really cares *that* much—he isn't that smart or good-looking (even though he makes megabucks on the market, she's certain her SAT scores were a few hundred points higher than his—and if his hairline is already receding at twenty-nine, what will it look like when he was forty?). But the more he ignores her, the more she wants him to call or e-mail. She is not that into him but for some reason, she wants him to be into her, just so she can turn him down.

## Choice C: The Booty Call

Good old Greg, aka Mr. Standby and Deliver. Like a sentry guarding a castle gate, Greg is always at the ready. Karen and Greg met online, at a dating site known to be somewhat "progressive" in its offerings. Their first meeting was more a playful affair than one filled with romance and the promise of a future, but sometimes that is just the way it goes, and it suited Karen just fine. This casual arrangement had been going on for more than a year, and by Karen's estimation, while it was not love, at least it was steady and there when she wanted it. She is thirty-three and feeling the effects of her prime. This pays the bills, so to speak.

And if she and Greg aren't exactly friends, they are friendly enough to fuck every few weeks or so. She thinks he is cute (and so do her friends), and he knows which buttons to push. And Karen feels empowered by having sex like a man, whenever she wants it, without any of the messy emotional aspects. Who needs a boyfriend to take care of, and all those obligations? All the guys she knew slept around and had meaningless (but decent) sex, and so could she. Her arrangement with Greg is proof that it's possible.

But work and her travel schedule are leaving her little free time of late, and it has been months since she and Greg have had one of their evenings. She is in the mood for some fun, and his text message earlier in the week had been an unexpected but welcome diversion from an otherwise tedious week of branding brainstorm sessions. Greg knew how to tantalize her with words, and their chats had a decidedly dirty flavor. For Karen, the lead-up and the raunchy chatting are a big part of the turn-on, and it is something she finds difficult to bring into her more serious relationships. But with Greg, she can let loose and be wild, and she finds that freedom exciting. There is no shyness or concern for what he might think the next day. In fact, there is usually no next day, as they rarely have sleepovers. Theirs is a relationship built on efficiency and mutual needs, nothing more. Neither is being deceived, and they are honest about the other aspects of their dating life. Karen doesn't care that Greg dates other women, so long as he is safe, clean, and available when she wants him.

And so it is that she finds herself driving to Greg's apartment in Lincoln Park at 10:15 P.M. on this particular Friday, her elegant La Perla lingerie covered by a knee-length wool skirt and a cream-colored tank top. They had long ago dispensed with the pretense of meeting at a bar, only to leave half-finished drinks on the table as they raced home to rip each other's clothes off. It's more honest to just show up and get down to business. And Karen loves the idea of appearing at his door with such a naughty purpose in mind (it was not dropping a mink coat to her ankles at a seedy motel, but it would do).

Upon her arrival, Greg undresses her slowly, taking time to admire all the work she has put into her outfit. But his delicacy soon turns to schoolboy fumbling, and within twenty minutes they have accomplished their mission. And while Karen did achieve orgasm during some of their sessions, tonight is not one of them. Somehow the idea of this affair is better than the actual sex. When it is over, Greg rushes out of bed to show her some new CDs and books he had bought. He has a habit of getting up immediately, to clean up his apartment or check his e-mail. She does not expect (or really want) any intimacy, though she is often ready for a second round of fun well before Greg is. So, she just lays there, looking at the scattered remnants of her outfit, feeling vacant and not particularly satisfied.

She dresses and gets ready to leave, despite Greg's assurance that he will back in business after a short rest. More than anything, she wants to take a shower, watch TV, and be alone. She'll have to finish the job Greg started, when she gets home (Greg is no match for the lavender Dolphin). Driving back, she begins to consider the wisdom of this quasi-relationship. If the sex is not even that great, what is the point? And was this casual arrangement at odds with what she really wanted from life? When she gets home she makes a vow to curtail things with Greg and to put an end to this casual arrangement. She upholds this vow for six weeks, until the Friday afternoon when she receives a deliciously dirty text message inviting her once again to the edge of sweet release.

Choices, choices, choices. Having choices is a luxury, and it's better than not having them. But the real challenge is how you use them.

part 2 THE MARKETPLACE

## 5. YOU'RE NOT THAT INTO HIM EITHER, BUT YOU'RE DATING HIM IN THE MEANTIME

*"Life moves pretty fast. If you don't stop and look around once and awhile you could miss it."*

—Ferris Bueller's Day Off

"I'm just dating him in the meantime." The sentiment reminds me of something Pablo Picasso said to aspiring artists: "Never take a part-time job because it will become your full-time life." Of course, being a painter, Picasso didn't mind starving a bit every now and again, unlike the rest of us hungry in-between mealers. Had Picasso been a therapist, however, he likely would have warned his women patients to forgo "dating in the meantime," since it so often leads to a full-time string of relationships with men they're not that into (Picasso would have said it in French, which might have made it sound more romantic).

"Art is the lie that tells the truth," Picasso also said,

a sentiment that applies as much to cubism as it does to dating. In other words, image is all. Let the thing speak for you and eventually it will speak for itself. The image will become the truth, leaving the motivation underlying it far behind and forgotten. But enough with the dead white men already, it's time to get back to reality.

## Time Is Not on Anyone's Side

> *"So I met this guy, and I knew he wasn't right for me but he was really persistent, and I was bored. After a while he started sleeping over. Pretty soon he was living with me, and people started asking, 'So are you engaged?' 'When are you getting married?' etc., etc. No one ever asked, 'Are you in love with him?' and I guess I avoided asking myself. After a while, we got engaged, stayed that way for two years, and never set a date. Finally, it was clear we were both settling. So we broke up. I'd love to tell you that I met a great guy who changed my life but the truth is last month I turned thirty-six, and I'm still on the dating treadmill."*
>
> —Connie, 36, real estate broker, New York

Dating "in the meantime" is based on the belief that time is infinite. But in reality, "in the meantime" is wasted time, which means missed opportunities. Sure, you may be living in the moment, but it's a moment that has been dulled around the edges, stripped of importance and immediacy. When you're living in meantime mode, you're constantly letting yourself off the hook and embracing a reactive approach to life rather than a proactive one.

"In the meantime" is the same as saying, "This is only for now. Someday things will be different." It's like putting your life on deferral indefinitely. Well, let me tell you, ladies: *Someday just arrived.* Someday is right now; it's realizing that you've lowered your standards and settled into a pattern of diminished expectations.

But it doesn't have to be that way. In my line of work, I meet plenty of couples, and you'd be amazed how many have found lasting love after getting out of an "in the meantime" relationship, often within months, even weeks, of being newly single. When I ask why they stayed with someone they knew was wrong for so long, many say they did it out of obligation, for friendship, or simply due to fear of being alone. Logistics also often come into play ("neither of us wanted to give up the apartment—it was rent-controlled") but it's never about love or passion. As long as you're living in the meantime, you'll never really know what you're missing. And by doing so, your life is just a rehearsal for a performance that never comes.

Dating someone in the meantime can also mean what my friend Marla calls "dating for dinner." Sure, it sounds comical but when women do this, they're settling. They become performers, showing up for their night on the town. They also become untrue to themselves, because they're putting on an act for the men they're trying to impress. Of course, the more they act, the less they become aware that they're probably not that into the guy they are out with.

These meantime men, in the meantime, give women a false sense of security. They create a certain level of comfort by making women feel better about themselves for being out on a not-so-hot date on a Saturday night rather than home alone eating a Lean Cuisine and watching a Lifetime movie.

## ARE YOU AFRAID OF YOU?

Autophobia is an abnormal and persistent fear of being alone. Autophobics often worry about being ignored and unloved. These days, we're probably all a little autophobic. How often do we define ourselves in terms of others? We're popular, we're respected, we're well liked, we're leaders, we're team players. We become dependent on others for a definition of ourselves.

Many of us have never spent any significant period of time alone. We go from our families to college to roommates and into relationships. We've become good at dealing with others but often at the expense of learning how to deal with ourselves. And in today's interconnected, technology-driven landscape (e-mail, text messaging, and cell phones), we can easily avoid that sort of internal dialogue and introspection that forces self-reflection and -realization.

Like getting a pet, dating becomes another form of insulating ourselves from being alone. When we date in the meantime, it's often because we're afraid of dealing with ourselves; we have lost the ability to judge ourselves without the intermediation of others' judgments of us.

## There and Now

*"For me it's the difference between going out on a Friday night and staying home. If I have nothing else going on, why not?"*

—Amelia, 33, fashion executive, Los Angeles

Meantimers don't live in the here and now, they live in the *there and now*. "In the meantime" is a defense. It's a way of hedging your bets and avoiding the very risks that often lead to personal growth. "In the meantime" people almost always have big plans: to get in shape, to sign up for some classes, to quit their jobs, to start that novel, to change their lives. The present is trivialized; it's the future that matters. All of the things they're not happy with are just for now. These same meantimers believe they hold the reins of their destiny by keeping a full social calendar.

But more than anything, "in the meantime" dating is motivated by fear. It may be the fear of confronting that guy you're dating, the fear of being alone, or the fear of having to go back to the singles scene and the dismal dating treadmill, but it's fear nonetheless. And that fear is preventing you from taking a needed step toward empowerment. Worse, that fear is keeping you in a state of limbo, and it's lowering the standards you're willing to tolerate.

Sometimes the "there and now" isn't about the future, it's about the past and not being able to move on, as in the case of Emily and her "remembrance of dates past:"

"Jonathan was my college boyfriend. I followed him to Los Angeles, moved in with him, and waited for him to ask me to marry him. But it never happened. Finally, we broke up, and I started seeing other guys, yet I couldn't help comparing them to Jonathan. My friends kept reminding me what an asshole he was and how badly he treated me but I held him up on this pedestal. He'll always be the one who got away, and I don't know if any guy will ever compare—even though he's paunchy and balding and married now. Still, part of me is just afraid of getting hurt like that again, and it's easier to stay in the past than deal with the present."

Emily may be looking backward, but she is still living "in the meantime," forsaking the present for some other point in time.

## The Boyfriend Mirror

*"When you're alone you don't feel as attractive, because there's no guy telling you how hot you are. You become dependent on that voice, and you develop a boyfriend imperative: You need to have one at all costs. Even if he's completely wrong, it's better than being alone."*

—Cathy, 35, marketing executive, Indianapolis

When I was a teenager, I could never understand women's magazines like *Cosmopolitan* and *Glamour* (why was I reading them in the first place? Good question). Considering that they catered to a female readership, it never made sense that the models were so perfect and artificial. Then it dawned on me: Magazines like *Playboy* are created for the male gaze, and magazines like *Cosmo* are created for women who view themselves through the male gaze. Women have internalized the male gaze, and it follows them everywhere.

This leads many women to a crisis in confidence, whereby their value is based on the judgment of all men, echoed by the man they happen to be dating. If they are not dating anybody, the problem intensifies. By reducing it to one man's judgment, they feel safer and more desirable to all men. And without that single male affirmation, they feel they have no value at all. Sometimes women date or have casual sex just to get that instant ego boost, to reduce all men to a single hard-on that tells them they're attractive and desirable even if it's just "for the meantime."

## The Bearable Lightness of Dating

*"When I was in my twenties, I used to go out with lots of guys who I never thought were right. I'd see them, hook up with them, sometimes even date them, but I always told myself he's just for now, Mr. Perfect is coming up. But you know what, I sort of got stuck because I wasn't putting myself out there to meet Mr. Perfect, but the ideal always made the other guys pale. I think back on some of those 'meantime' guys, and maybe they were Mr. Right."*

—Amy, 35, stockbroker, Phoenix

Imagine going through years of your life with the gut feeling that none of it really matters *yet,* that it will start at some point in the future, and that the present doesn't really count. Does this feeling seem familiar? Have you ever told yourself that everything will ultimately fall into place once you [fill in the blank, e.g., publish that book, lose ten pounds, meet a great guy, get that promotion, get your own column, buy that apartment, show 'em all, and so on]? Who wouldn't wind up numbed to real hope and possibility after exerting so much energy for stuff that really doesn't matter? And who wouldn't want to convince themselves that at least some of the effort was worthwhile, that all of the energy you expended on that asshole you sometimes call your boyfriend (when you're not calling him worse), actually did matter?

This is not to say you need only live in the moment. That's impossible, at least according to Milan Kundera, who called this the "unbearable lightness of being." We can't live every moment like it's our last because doing so would make every moment too serious. So we do the opposite. We live lightly and frivolously, squandering our moments. This is best illustrated in dating scenarios, which translates into hooking up and settling, and allowing life to pass us by.

But if we're not supposed to live in the moment, what should we do? The best course, while not easy, is to find a happy medium between the two—essentially living comfortably in the now while not forsaking the moment by treating it as the "meantime." Confusing, huh? I call it the Bearable Lightness of Dating (BLD), and I suppose it's a way of thinking more than a true course of action. But you're the one who's called upon, and you're the one who must be aware of your actions and your intentions.

When it comes to BLD, you have to determine whether the guy you're dating has, at a bare minimum, the potential to be a true in-the-moment guy. If he's solely a meantime man, the burden is on you to cut the cord right now. You can't put it off. Life is too precious to get stuck in an endless cycle of meantimers who will never, ever wind up with you in the here and now.

## Are Your Standards Too High?: In the Meantime, in Disguise

> *"I meet a lot of guys, but it's harder and harder to find one who has all the qualities I want. If he's not slightly balding, then he's divorced, or worse, in his late thirties and still single. Or he's none of these but there is something about his shoes that's just not right."*
>
> —Jane, 36, chief marketing officer, New York

One of the potential results of realizing that you're dating "in the meantime" and taking action is being alone. This can be a fearful step but it's worth taking since it can only lead to strength and empowerment. While it may be difficult to do, it's necessary if you're really going to reach for the love you deserve.

But just as you have to be aware when you're with someone for the wrong reasons, you need to assess whether you're alone because you know what you want and refuse to settle or because your standards have grown impossibly high. Knowing yourself is healthy and, of course, I'm encouraging you to raise your standards. But along with these standards comes an ability to be realistic. That means eventually settling down with a man who, like most of us guys, has some flaws.

Seeking perfection is another way of living in the meantime, only it's from the opposite side of the continuum. You're still forsaking the present ("real" dating opportunities that might not meet your impossibly high expectations) for the future (perfection will arrive soon). It's a matter of your own self-awareness. Now, I'm not telling you to settle for less than you deserve. There is a difference between perfectionism and knowing what you want. It's the difference between rejecting a guy because his shoes are wrong and realizing that you have different views on raising children. Sure, shoes are important but is it enough of a reason to write someone off? As you'll learn later, thankfully for me, my wife was able to see past my own footwear faults.

## The Flip Side: Blinded by the Meantime

*"I don't have six months anymore to let a guy show me who he is. I can't waste that kind of time. If I don't feel it after the third date, he's a meantime man, and I'm an out-of-time woman."*

—Melissa, 34, publishing, Seattle

There is a subtle but important difference between dating "in the meantime" and taking enough time to know whether you might really like a guy. One of the points of this chapter is to make you aware that you might be settling. But I would urge you to do so without being overly guarded. As suggested above, the Bearable Lightness of Dating is a good medium.

The problem with being too guarded is that you're never going to give a guy a chance. You have to at least commit to finding out who he is. Now, that might happen on the first date or it might take several months. It's up to you but I'm just urging you not to be too quick to judge. If your "in the meantime" radar is set too high, you've already set yourself up to believe that this is just something to do until the real romance begins. This could be *the* guy but you're predisposed not to see it or believe it. If neon signs were flashing HE'S THE ONE in your face, you'd probably avert your eyes to the blinding light and walk away none the wiser.

In other words, be cautious of when you think you might be settling for a protracted meantimer but don't be so blinded that you write off every man you meet.

## Be Honest

As funk legend Morris Day used to sing, "What time is it?" While his standard answer was "Time to get wild and loose," you need to apply this question to your dating life. If your answer is "in the meantime," make an assessment. As with casual sex, it may be okay to have an occasional few dates or casual sex with a meantimer.

But don't forget that enough "in the meantimes" could add up to a lot of lost time and confusion. Sure, you're probably learning as you go, and maybe the sex is not that bad. But are you dating him because you want to or because you need to (*i.e.*, is he only there to remind you that you're attractive and worthwhile until the real thing comes along)? If it's fear that's keeping you there "in the meantime," you're cheating yourself out of other opportunities, both for personal growth and for meeting other potential mates. Like nicotine and reality TV watching, "in the meantime" can be habit-forming. Whether it's holding onto that fuck buddy, dating a guy who's not right, or simply dating just to date, it'll creep up on you and eventually become an addiction of sorts. More important, you may convince yourself there's something real between you just to avoid the fact that you've been exerting so much energy for something that doesn't count. And then the guy you never meant to be the one may wind up becoming the one.

## Raise (Your Standards) and Reach (for Love)

- **Listen to Pablo:** Don't get caught in the part-time rut . . . it becomes the full-time soon enough.
- **Turn "the meantime" into *"real*-time":** Make it count; make it real. If you're lowering your standards and wasting your time, you may be missing out on a real chance for love. Make now matter while making the meantime *meaningful*.
- **Tread lightly:** Find the balance between living every moment as if it were the last with always believing tomorrow will bring what you want. Live for today but keep an eye on tomorrow.
- **Get real:** Having standards is great but don't set the bar so high that nobody will ever be able to leap over it. Being unrealistic is another form of "in the meantime." If you think a maybe guy might actually be an in-the-moment guy, then don't shunt him away as a meantimer. Relationships take time. Despite the fact that your biological and emotional clocks are ticking, you owe it to

yourself to give him the time he needs to prove himself or hang himself.

- **Lower the drawbridge:** Don't get taken advantage of, but don't play your cards so close to your chest that you miss out on some great opportunities.

*"Most women use more brains picking a horse in the third at Belmont than they do picking a husband."*

—*How to Marry a Millionaire*

*B*lues singer Bessie Smith divinely expressed the sentiment in 1927 that "A Good Man Is Hard to Find," alternately known as "a hard man is good to find" (a more difficult task in the pre-Viagra days). That being said, the lack of good men has been touted by most of the women I've interviewed as the chief reason for dating so many "meantimers." But frankly, I don't think you women are doing yourselves justice.

If we men are falling short of your reasonable expectations, why should you validate our inadequate behavior by "settling"? In fact, let me cross the great sex divide and venture further: Perhaps it's high time you women staged a *boy*cott. For those of us *boys* who are failing to meet minimal standards of dating decency (out of laziness, lack of effort, indifference), just say no to *cott*ing down altogether. Stop positively reinforcing the bad behavior and, believe me, we'll start picking up the slack.

To put it another way, if the quality of your favorite restaurant suddenly declined, would you still continue to pay $14.95 for a rancid goat cheese salad? Wouldn't you take your business elsewhere or, if all else failed, cook for yourself? Well, if we men are falling short of your expectations, maybe it's high time you boycotted our business as well and eat where the getting's good.

## Is a Good Man *That* Hard to Find?

> *"From a distance, it seems like there are plenty of guys out there. I mean, I see them on the streets. So, why can't I find one to date? I always end up with a guy I'm just not that wild about."*
>
> —Karen, 33, antiques dealer, Chicago

So, do Bessie Smith's words still hold true? Perhaps. But let's look at whether it's an issue of quantity or quality. From a pure population standpoint, there's no shortage of available men out there. One hundred five boys are born for every one hundred girls. Among those aged thirty to thirty-four, there are four single men for every three single women. That means you could get rid of 25 percent of the single men—and I'm sure plenty of candidates come to mind—in that age bracket, and there still would be a man for every woman, unless you happen to live in New York City, where the ratios are sadly reversed (hey, if you can make out here, you'll make out anywhere—yeah, I know, bad pun).

So, there is no genuine shortage of men per se. What you are really complaining about is not lack of quantity but lack of quality. If you're complaining, it's probably a good sign. It means you're not willing to settle for a guy you're just not into. You'd rather wait for the right one than date someone simply for the sake of dating. And as we'll discover in the next section, the reason it may seem like there are so few good men out there is because women are, as you've always suspected, smarter, more mature, and far more capable of healthy relationships in terms of emotional and sexual capacity.

## Your Incredibly Growing Standards

> *"I've spent a lot time working on myself, and I feel like I deserve somebody who has done the same and who, frankly, is worth my energy."*
>
> —Samantha, 37, pediatrician, New York

So, what gives? Why have so many of you decided that the men out there are, basically, no damn good? Well, while men may not have changed as much as one would have liked since 1927, women have. Your standards have been raised over the years. And what was considered "good enough" or even "great" for your mom or grandmother just doesn't cut it for you anymore (sorry, Grandpa). You're smarter, better educated, and more successful than ever before. What that means is you're no longer looking for a protector or a provider but a partner on equal footing.

Women now make up the majority of college undergraduates in most four-year colleges and universities. Women run corporations and even governments. And it's because of this independence that women have choices. And more and more women are choosing to stay single rather than settle for second best.

These advances have emotional consequences. Most of today's women are not itching to settle down right after college. Like your male peers, you want to travel the world and see what life has to offer. You want to date and experience new things, romantically and sexually. More pragmatic than your foremothers, you are choosing to live with a guy before accepting a proposal or foregoing the marriage part altogether, at least for a while. Then, all of a sudden, the years of cultural stereotypes come and bite you in the, umm, cranium.

Somehow, at a certain point, today's woman finds herself in an epic crisis when she hits her thirties and finds she is still single. Sure, she may have achieved any number of professional and personal milestones but the window of opportunity for getting married and having children, which once seemed to be so wide open, is now inching shut. Yes, you're in better shape, healthier, and have better access to medicine than your parents, but still, your eggs have a shelf life.

So, you're on the hunt for a man, one who's as good as you are (as if that were possible)—successful, attractive, educated, serious. And why the hell shouldn't you want that?

But it seems like so many of the good guys, at least the ones who look good on paper, aren't nearly as impressed with your qualifications as you thought they might be. They are happier to coast along with the hot young receptionist than go head-to-head with the woman who just made partner.

And as men have rested on their laurels (usually watching sports), women have been using this time to become, well, better at just about everything (better read, more cultured, well-rounded, more socially and politically involved, you name it). The problem with finding a good man is that you've gotten way too good for us.

## Being Smart Means Being Patient

> "Preparing for domesticity is at first breezy and exciting: The streets are filled with all sorts of terrific houses (and men), and the choices seem limitless. It's only when you get to the point of purchase that real estate (or romance) reveals its heartbreaking propensities. . . . It's hard to find the mix of qualities you think you deserve. . . . Houses with 'potential' mean years of wearisome renovation. And that place with the fabulous view? It has been on the market too long; there must be something wrong with it."
>
> —*Wall Street Journal*, January 3, 2003

Social conservatives and other narrow-minded folks will tell you that this house-hunting analogy is what third-wave feminism reaped. Basically, you've gotten what you deserve. You spent too much time focused on education, career, sexual exploits, and having fun, and now you want to have your cake and eat it too, only to find it's too late. You can post on the Internet personals and speed-date all you want but you made this lonely procrustean bed: The trade-off for trying to be so independent is that you've meanwhile missed your chance to find a man. The good ones were swept up by the more conservative girls, and now all you can do is lower your standards or stay single forever.

But let me just say this to all of you loud and clear: Bullshit!

According to Barbara Dafoe Whitehead, codirector of the National Marriage Project at Rutgers University, women who wait longer to marry are more mature, more financially secure, and have a better sense of who they could happily spend their lives with than those who marry early. Moreover, studies have shown that later marriages tend to be "unusually stable and long-lasting." So, maybe the adage that "good things come to those who wait" is true.

Whitehead also points out that women with college degrees are actually more likely to marry and less likely to get divorced. "We predict that marriage levels will be highest for those women who are, in theory, most able to live well alone—the most highly educated," concluded a recent Princeton University study. And I can tell you that my own experience as a therapist, as well my choice to marry a woman way smarter than me, has supported this.

Social conservatives will also point to biology to back their spiteful claims, suggesting that you're past your prime. They will say a woman is most nubile and "marriageable" in her late teens and early twenties, and that men are conditioned to seek women of that age for physical and Darwinian reasons, regardless of how intelligent, educated, financially well-established, success-ful, and otherwise accomplished those older women are.

Are there really men who, when faced with a choice between an independent, attractive, self-sufficient thirtysomething (or fortysomething) woman and one who is younger but more de-pendent and less emotionally evolved, will choose the latter? Yes, of course. But does this result in there being fewer available men to meet the expectations of the older, more mature, independent woman? Not really, unless you'd actually want to date that sort of man in the first place.

In a way, this makes the market more efficient because it gets rid of the sort of men who have a propensity for the young and dependent. The truth is, you'd never be into those kinds of men to begin with—so let them go lead their shallow little lives. Don't put down the women. Put down the men.

## THE "THERE ARE NO GOOD MEN LEFT" EXCUSES CHART

Pick the complaint that most applies to you when you chant the mantra that "There Are No Good Men Left":

### Because They've Been Taken by Your Friends

One of my patients continually developed crushes on her friends' and sisters' husbands, which led to her having sexual fantasies about them. Part of my job was to bring her back to reality. But her problem was based on her perception that these other women had "taken" all the good men.

### And Any Man Who's Still Single Must Be "Damaged Goods"

This is a common theme among women that I treat, though sort of just desserts for the decades of spinster derision. They believe that if a guy is still on the market past age thirty-five, there must be something wrong with him. "If he's so great, why hasn't someone else married him?" they wonder. Well, perhaps you are that someone else.

### So I Have to Date the Ones Who Are Not So Good

Do you? Not really. Not if you're self-aware and keep your standards aligned with what you truly want from a relationship. If you're dating just to date, you're settling, and you're making it harder to find the good ones and easier for the not-so-good ones to stay not-so-good.

### Because Even the Good Ones Are Not That Great

This is a variation on the idea that "all men are pigs." And while it may be based on your own very valid experiences, it's globalizing a belief based on some specific instances.

### So I'm Going to Live a Life of Quiet Celibacy with My Cats

Hmmm. It worked for Mother Teresa but if you're at this stage in the dating cycle, you're probably feeling defeated and even defensive. If this is the life you really want, well, good luck with those hairballs. If it's not, you need to get back on the horse and scout some new canyons.

## Good Men Do Exist (You Just May Not Be Seeing Them)

> *"While I do enjoy dating and I'm all right with being single, a big part of me craves domesticity and just having one person to come home to. I know I cannot rush it, however."*
>
> —Paul, 35, advertising copywriter, Minneapolis

I meet good men all the time who are single and ready to be in something "real." They get as bummed out about bad setups, singles' nights, and Internet dating as you do. They may not be facing the same pressures but their desire for a meaningful, significant relationship is there. And like you, they have visited the buffet table often enough to know the value of a home-cooked meal.

As I mentioned in the last chapter, many men are taking more time to enjoy bachelorhood. And while some of this is inspired by a desire to date and have fun, these same men are aware that the time they spend learning about themselves will also make them better husbands and fathers. So, where are these men and why aren't you meeting them? I'm not sure—perhaps they're too busy doing yoga or taking cooking classes. Or perhaps you're not attracted to them, so ingrained is the desire for the misbehaving alpha male that his more evolved metrosexual counterpart gets derided by the media as less desirable.

A more recent trend that's affecting relationships is directly related to an increase in financial independence among women: While some men are threatened by a woman whose salary is equal to or greater than their own, others are looking for a partner to share economic responsibilities. Such men are not "reverse gold diggers." Rather, they are simply aware of the realities of raising a family in today's economically challenging environment.

So what is the big secret? Well, it's about finding a man who is ready and being more creative about where you look for him. Insanity can be defined as doing the same thing over and over and expecting different results. Are you doing that? Going to bars, asking the same set of friends if they know any eligible men, looking through the same online personals? Does that make you insane? Not yet. But if you keep doing that and telling yourself there are no good men out there, you're sure to drive yourself crazy.

## The Flip Side: Water, Water Everywhere!

> *"I constantly find myself in situations where I have to choose between two guys, or where I am dating a few men at one time. I get hit on constantly and I love the attention. I'm just not sure how to narrow it down."*
>
> —Julie, 27, legal assistant, Atlanta

While a lot of you might wish you had Julie's "problem," her situation is probably born of insecurity, not a surplus of viable options. Some women (and men) simply need the attention that dating provides, and they tend to date en masse, complaining about all the options they have as they laugh all the way to the ego bank. However, in many of these cases, it's not a situation of too many overadequate men but rather one of lots of inadequate male gazing.

Such women are "overdaters." They settle not out of a shortage of men but out of a lack of focus or standards altogether. Overdaters are always in search of a few good men but what qualifies the men as good is related more to their presence than it is to their personalities.

## Be Honest

Settling for some guy you're not that into because you think all the goods are taken (or never existed to begin with) is a little bit like accepting defeat before the game is over. It's like going back to that same awful restaurant time and again when there are plenty of better options just around the corner. There are decent men out there who want the same things you do. And in the end, it takes only one. So stop paying premium prices for poor quality and take a look at what else is around. And if you don't like what you find for the time being, there's nothing wrong with cooking for one.

## Raise (Your Standards) and Reach (for Love)

- **Where the boys are:** Mathematically, there are enough men to go around. Are they all for you? No. But you can't get away with the excuse that there are too few good men. You need to look in different places. And you need to stop positively reinforcing bad behavior. Instead of hitting the bar, raise it.
- **Too successful for your own good:** No, not really. But due to advances in your career and emotional freedoms, the type of man you're looking for seems harder to come by. Still, that does not mean you should lower your standards.
- **But . . .**

- **Keep the door open:** Some women get hung up on standards or what was drilled into our heads by our parents ("marry a nice doctor"). Don't lower your expectations but make sure you're casting a wide enough net.
- **Wait your turn:** Being patient is hard but the more you get to know yourself, the more likely you are to find the right relationship, one that works the first time. And that's definitely something worth waiting for.
- **Men want the same things:** Okay. So, maybe men have a little more freedom in terms of age and timing. So what? There are plenty of men out there who want exactly what you do.

## 7. YOU'RE NOT THAT INTO HIM EITHER, BUT ALL YOUR FRIENDS ARE GETTING MARRIED

*"They're either married or gay. And if they're not gay, they've just broken up with the most wonderful woman in the world, or they've just broken up with a bitch who looks exactly like me. They're in transition from a monogamous relationship and they need more space. Or they're tired of space, but they just can't commit. Or they want to commit, but they're afraid to get close. They want to get close, you don't want to get near them."*

—*The Big Chill*

*I*f I had to do it all over again, I'd own a mill that made the paper used for wedding invitations. I almost need a separate office to keep track of all the invites I get from friends, family, and colleagues—and I'm not even that popular a guy. It's overwhelming, this business of marriage. And when you get to a certain age, it seems like you receive an invite every week.

As it turns out, all of your friends are either married or engaged. *All of them,* even the ones who never had boyfriends in college; even the ones you were not sure even liked boys. Hell, some of them are already going on seconds! Oh, look, there's the mail carrier now carrying another batch of cream-colored envelopes bearing calligraphic type. Here comes the bride again, and she's not you.

If you're like a lot of women in their late twenties and thirties, your friends' wedding announcements leave you with mixed feelings: You're genuinely excited for them, of course, but you're also slightly envious. Why does your friend get to wear a gorgeous Vera Wang gown while you're stuck in a puke green polyester bridesmaid's dress? When your friends get married, you're reminded once again of just how single you are.

Do your friends' marriage plans leave you feeling pressured to date or stay with someone you're not that into? Do you feel like you need to "catch up," losing sight of the fact that the goal shouldn't simply be to marry but to marry someone you'll want to spend the rest of your life with?

Let me ease your mind or at least, your sense of envy: Many of your married friends will be single again (as you may know, the percentage of first marriages that end in divorce is about 50 percent, and the percentage of remarriages that end in divorce is about 60 percent). These odds are definitely not helped when many women, like yourself, succumb to the sense of social pressure and get hitched to whomever they happen to be dating when they reach (or, heaven forbid, surpass) the age of thirty. By doing this, you're focusing on the endpoint of marriage rather than choosing an ideal mate, and it's a disaster in the making.

As a sex therapist in my mid-thirties, young married couples are my bread and butter. And I can tell you that the only thing worse than being single and miserable is being married and miserable. If you lower your standards now, you'll be paying for it in years to come. Of course, it's easy for me to say that. I'm a married man. But despite that, I understand that society and even biology start to weigh in pretty heavily as you drift out of your happy-go-lucky twenties into your are-you-really-still-single? thirties.

## HOW FED UP ARE YOU?

Match your feeling with each of the various scenarios by placing the appropriate letter in the corresponding circle:

a) Fed up
b) Very fed up
c) Not so much fed up as over it
d) As mad as Martha Stewart on arraignment day

- ☐ Getting fitted for yet another purple taffeta dress that you will wear only once
- ☐ Being an "aunt" in thirteen states
- ☐ Having married friends tell you how envious they are of your "freedom"
- ☐ All those goddamned fancy strollers
- ☐ Girls' Night Out turning into the Look at My Lactating Breasts Club

☐ Deciding whether to pay your rent or buy that expensive engagement/wedding/baby/second baby/housewarming present you "owe" your friend

☐ Your mother and her one question

☐ Minivan ads

## The Race for the Ring

> *"If I were married, my life would be so much more fulfilling. I'm tired of dating. I want the real thing."*
>
> —Margo, 28, teacher, San Francisco

Let me start off with a caveat to this chapter: I want you to be married, but only if that's what you want. There's nothing wrong with your desire to have that storybook wedding, an adoring husband, two well-behaved children, and a feisty dog who chews on the legs of the heirloom sofa in your sparkling center-hall colonial (surrounded by a white picket fence, if that's what makes you tick). So, keep in mind that the divorce statistics above and the scenarios I'll present in this chapter are intended to help you get what you want, not swear off your dreams of white tulle and ice sculptures altogether.

That said, the rush to the altar often eclipses the big picture (happiness, finding the right partner, and spiritual sanity) for many women, and when you're single it's easy to think that marriage will mysteriously change *everything*. Of course, the truth is that it doesn't, and the women who think that way are the ones who push those divorce statistics even higher. Marriage takes work. It's harder than being single, even in the best of circumstances when the relationship is on solid ground.

Your wedding day may be a storybook affair but marriage isn't just one day. When you exchange vows, you're supposed to be in it for the long haul. So, if you can't see past the reception hall or the honeymoon in Paris (or even all that great crystal and china from your gift registry), you might be getting married for the wrong reason.

Your family wants to see you married. But while they may have the best of intentions (yes, they do think you could be happy with their best friend's insurance agent's oldest son), their nagging can lead you to make some bad decisions. And the forty-eight magazines solely devoted to the walk down the aisle in a shimmering white satin-and-lace dress? They probably don't care that much about you, but their advertisers sure are interested in perpetuating the very costly business of marriage. It probably seems as if everywhere you turn, the media is bombarding you with the image of marriage as the ultimate life goal and the antidote to all that is wrong with your life.

You have to learn to drown out the clamor that society is foisting upon you to be married. Accept it, laugh at it, and understand it, but don't let it be the sole arbiter of your actions. You do have a say in the matter, even if it seems like everyone is telling you that you need to be married by, oh, next month or so.

## The Baby Brigade

> *"Every time I read a magazine I'm told that if I don't have a baby by the time I'm thirty-five, it'll never happen. When I do the math, that means I need to be married by thirty-three and have had met the guy by the time I'm thirty."*
>
> —Patricia, 32, magazine editor, New York

First comes love, then comes marriage, then comes the baby in the baby carriage. Of course, that makes sense on paper but it's a little trickier in real life. For some women, the pressure to get married is more biological than it is societal. The desire to have children is, of course, one of the strongest natural impulses a woman can feel. And despite our progressiveness as a culture, for most women, the first step to this is marriage (of course, there are other options; see the sidebar on page 87). But the key ingredient to the equation is finding someone you want to build a life and a family with.

Sometimes a woman's biological desires may be so overpowering, however, that they impair her ability to make the right choice with regard to a husband. Sure, he *can* father a child but should he?

The cliché of the ticking biological clock is so prevalent that it almost seems too obvious to mention. But it's a cliché for a reason. And mentioned in the last chapter, "in the meantime" can be wasted time. Let me give it to you straight here: Despite the odd story about fifty-something-year-old women giving birth to twins, the truth is that you do not have forever. *But* you certainly have plenty of good baby-breeding years past the age of thirty-five. While you may not have all the time in the world, you do have the time—no, the obligation—to make the right personal choices. Don't let biology push you into staying with a guy you're not that into. Dating someone you're not into is one thing but marrying them is quite another.

## AND BABY MAKES TWO

Science-fiction scenarios love to portray a future world in which, due to the advent of sperm banks and vibrators, men are suddenly irrelevant and relegated to the margins of servitude. Cinematic dystopias notwithstanding, I'm meeting more and more women who want to have babies and are happily going it alone. They have the money and maturity to support their goals. Sure, they'd prefer to have husbands, and they recognize the challenges of raising a child on their own, but the desire for motherhood supersedes everything else. Medical advances have made this possible, and an endless litany of cultural examples (from Murphy Brown to Angelina Jolie) have made it right.

My mom was an old-school single mother. Without infrastructure or support or understanding, she was judged rather than celebrated. She was an oddball, going against the grain of society. Today, marketers and politicians recognize the single mom as an important demographic, and my prediction is that third-wave feminism will produce/support single women having kids outside of any relationship with a man. With the same access to money and opportunities as a man, not only can a woman have sex like a man, she can have a baby without a man. Will this reality help to ease the pressure on women to marry in order to have children? We can only hope so.

# It's *Not* Raining Men

> *"I want to get married but I think it's more important to find someone I really want to be with. I'm willing to wait and, fortunately, as a man, I can."*
>
> —Michael, 36, lawyer, Philadelphia

You're a single woman who has a successful career, a healthy outlook on life, and a desire to settle down. You've done your share of dating, and you know what you're looking for in a man. So where the hell is he? Well, he's probably not that far away but, unfortunately, you may not be on the same page. There's no shortage of men who want to sleep with you but there is a drought when it comes to men who actively want to get married.

According to a recent study by the National Marriage Project at Rutgers University, men are waiting longer and longer to get married (surprise!). This study explored attitudes on sex, dating, meeting women, living together, marrying a soul mate, the timing of marriage, social pressures to marry, divorce, desire for children, and the work/family balance.

The median age of first marriage for men has reached twenty-seven, the highest age in our nation's history, according to the report. And why are men waiting so long to get married? Mainly because they can. According to the data collected, the reasons break down into five general areas.

Do any of these grossly stereotyped but accurate profiles sound like the men you know (and date)?

**Mr. Why Buy the Cow?** Men in this category are aware that, thanks to all that sexual empowerment and all those women out there having casual sex, their ability to get laid without getting married is easier today than it has ever been. So what's the hurry to settle down?

**Mr. Won't Go Changing:** These men have gotten too settled into their single ways and fear that marriage will require too many changes and compromises (such as food in the fridge and frilly dust ruffles on their beds).

**Mr. Perfect Ten:** This guy is waiting for the perfect soul mate, and she hasn't yet appeared, so he's willing to wait a little longer. Will he date you "in the meantime"? Sure, since he can probably afford to wait a little bit longer.

**Mr. Life in the Fast Lane:** A relic of the swinging seventies, these men want to enjoy the swinging-single life as long as they can. Look for the telltale ponytail and red sports car, and run, don't walk, to the nearest exit.

**Mr. Mama's Boy:** Ah, yes. This particular breed of single man is perhaps the most complex. A Freudian case study, he is seeking a mother, not a partner. If you don't mind doing his laundry and running his life, this may be the guy for you.

I'm not saying that all men are disinclined to get married. What all of the above evidence seems to indicate, however, is that men are extending their bachelor years. They are becoming choosier. And this is one of those bad news/good news situations.

The bad news is that this means the market is smaller and that there may be fewer available men. And those that are available are hemming and hawing and unwilling to commit (surprised? I didn't think so).

Fine, so what's the good news?

Well, the good news is that, in a way, this means that those men who do want to get married are doing so for the "right" reasons. Because they can get all the "other" stuff without getting married (sex, mainly), when they do get married, it's usually for something that can't be found as easily on the open market: love. Yes, I'm going out on a limb here and suggesting that there are guys out there who do want to get married, and they want to do so because, like you, the happily-ever-after stuff sounds, well, sorta nice.

What does all this mean for women? Men are shopping for very well-rounded mates (not in the Bridget Jones sense, but perhaps). And as shoppers get more discerning, the merchandise needs to be better. And no, I'm definitely not suggesting implants. I'm talking about getting beyond the packaging to the real stuff through self-exploration and learning to become a better partner, friend, and lover.

## The Marrying Kinds

> *"Beth is a very down-to-earth girl but once she got engaged, she became a total bridezilla. It made me want to stay single for a loooong time."*
>
> —Daniella, 31, writer, Boston

Now, to be fair, because I presented some of the male stereotypes above, I'm going to examine some of the more pointed female profiles below. Do you fit into one of these categories? Do your friends?

You may not even be aware that you fit into one of these categories. But the pressure to marry can do funny things to women.

**Ms. Wedding Planner:** She has been dreaming of a white wedding since she was eight years old and has it planned down to the last hydrangea. She has replayed her walk down the aisle a million times, and she had her soundtrack picked out before she knew who she was going to marry. At this point, the man is an afterthought and an accessory to the whole affair.

**Ms. I'd Never Give Up My Name:** She thinks marriage is no different from prostitution, and she'd never trade in her torn Lilith Fair T-shirt for a silly silk gown. She tells everyone she's not any man's property and defines herself in terms of not getting married.

**Ms. Golden Girl:** Straight from her loving (or not-so-loving) family into the arms of a protective husband, she's afraid to be on her own. She needs the security and comfort of marriage, both in material and emotional terms. You may see this type driving down the road in a fancy new SUV, on her way to Williams-Sonoma.

**Ms. Swinging Bachelorette:** Like Mr. Life in the Fast Lane, the bachelorette is all about having fun. Marriage may be on her mind but her actions don't imply that. Is she truly an empowered third-wave feminist having sex like a man, or do her swinging ways mask some deeper issues?

**Ms. Sexy Divorcée:** Fresh from a "starter marriage," the sexy divorcée is back in the dating game and happy to have an array of choices. In the best scenario, her first marriage will make her a more realistic candidate because the fantasy has already been demystified.

## You Think, Therefore You're Single (or, at Least, Unmarried)

> *"Marriage doesn't hold the mystique for me that it seems to hold for my friends. And I'd never want the attention of a big marriage. If I ever do it, I'll elope to some desert island."*
>
> —Paula, 33, bookkeeper, Seattle

Not every one of you will choose to get married. It's a simple fact. And if you don't, it doesn't mean you're a spinster or an old maid. If you've made the choice, for whatever reason, that marriage is not for you, then bravo. It takes courage to stand up to conventional wisdom and to decide against an institution that is so culturally ingrained.

Perhaps you're the child of a nasty divorce and, having seen the results of a marriage gone awry, you're turned off by the whole thing. This is a very sad and real state of affairs for many women, and there's no reason to feel self-conscious about such a decision. It's your life.

For others, marriage is simply a semantic state of affairs. They look, act, and feel married but they just don't have the piece of paper to prove it. Maybe you have a life partner and you want to spend your life together but don't feel the need to spend upwards of $35,000 to show the world how much you love each other.

And of course, maybe you just feel happier on your own. Sure, if the right guy were to come along, you'd consider getting married. But in a healthy way, you've accepted that it may not happen, and you're okay with that. So long as that decision is not passive or defeatist ("there are no good ones left," "no man will ever find me attractive," "I've just been hurt too many times before," and so on), it's a very honest and constructive choice.

As with so many things in life, it's often when you're not looking that you'll wind up finding exactly what you wanted all along (even if you weren't sure what that was in the first place). But that's no excuse for never leaving your apartment. You just need to realize that there are some things that are out of your control and other things that are within your reach.

## The Flip Side: Women Get Cold Feet Too!

> *"I love my boyfriend but it's like the tables are turned. He's the one pressuring me, and I'm sitting there saying, um, 'I'm just not ready to be Mrs. So-and-So yet.'"*
>
> —Melissa, 28, advertising, Chicago

So, you're living with a nice, sweet man. He's good to you, he is sane, and he even enjoys a good Crate and Barrel catalog every now and then. There's just one problem: He wants to get married—and soon. You want to get married too—well, eventually, in theory. But you're nervous. What if he's not the one? What if things change? What if there's some guy out there, living in

Guatemala and teaching English, whom you're destined to meet in two years? What if, what if, what if?

Not all women buy into the marriage myth. If you have cold feet, it might mean you're taking the time to think things through. And that's great. It means you're seeing past the hype of marriage (and all those bridal shower gifts), assessing the man you're with, and deciding whether you're really right for each other.

But similar to the "in the meantimer" whose expectations are way too high, you need to be sure you're not being unrealistic. Maybe your true soul mate *is* in South America; if so, you should wait. But if your south-of-the-border dreams are just a way of avoiding intimacy, it might be problematic. Your standards should be high but not impossible. As with being too much of a perfectionist, this is a subtle difference, and it is a matter of degree. But if you find that your standards are becoming ways to shield you from intimacy, they may be bordering on impossibly high.

## Be Honest

You want to get married. That's great. But are you dating the guy you're with because you really want to be with him for the rest of your life or because other pressures are making you feel like you need to find a husband? If you're on the path to marriage and you know deep down that you're not completely into the guy, it's going to be a long road. And the farther down that road you get, the harder it will be to find an exit.

Even today, marriage is presented as the golden bow on the

package of a meaningful life—the first step toward having a family and living happily ever after. Of course, a lot of women get there, only to find out that there's no happy in that "ever after."

## Raise (Your Standards) and Reach (for Love)

- **Walk, don't run:** Getting married can be a goal but you need not pursue it at the cost of finding the right man. If you're with him simply because he can get you across the finish line, you're in the race for the wrong reasons.
- **First things first:** Yes, biology is powerful, but don't be blinded by baby madness. You have time, and your children will be *much* better off if you make the right choice in a husband and potential father.
- **Take time for you:** Men have time and freedom, and they're getting more selective. Instead of dating Mr. In-Between, spend some time getting to know yourself.
- **Single is not a dirty word:** Being single is not a disease, and marriage is certainly not a cure for anything. If you're not married, for whatever reason, embrace that choice, and don't listen to the naysayers.
- **Aim high, but be realistic:** If you're not ready for the ring, maybe you've not met the right guy. Be true to yourself and your standards but make sure they are not superhuman.

*M*ichelle is a thirty-one-year-old architect who lives in San Francisco. The daughter of Korean immigrants, she was raised in a traditional background. Her modern tendencies frustrate her parents (her choice to pursue architecture is at odds with their wishes), and they feel that, by now, she should be married with children, and they do not hesitate to share this with her. Michelle struggles with reconciling her background with her more Americanized views. She prides herself on her independence and her adventurous spirit. And while she finds her parents' perspectives old-fashioned, deep down she believes they might be right, and she cannot figure out why she is single. And the weddings of all her friends, which seem to happen weekly, only serve to remind her of this. Now she must decide what to do about her friend Cathy's wedding in New York. She and Cathy were roommates in college but it's been almost a decade since they really spent quality time together. Still, Cathy has asked Michelle to be in the wedding party (she is having one of those large processions, so making the cut is not a tremendous honor). To add to her list of decisions, Michelle is invited with a date, despite the fact that she does not have a serious boyfriend.

Michelle has the following options. She can:

**a)** Go to the wedding alone and just deal with it.

**b)** Go to the wedding and take Paul, a perfectly nice but not quite right in-betweener she is dating.

**c)** Go to the wedding and try to win a bet she has with a group of her single friends in San Francisco that one of them can find a random guy and convince him to attend the wedding with her, posing as her fiancé.

**d)** Decline the invitation, stay home, and spend the weekend thinking of ways to spam the author of this book.

Since you already know the gimmick, I can't really ask you to do this test, but we're going to leave the box, just in case you want to go through the motions. Again, for those who wish to do so, please make your selection and then, in twenty words or less, explain why you made the choice.

## PLEASE WORK IN THIS BOX

—DO NOT TURN PAGE UNTIL YOU HAVE
COMPLETED THIS TEST—
(Or do what you want. You know where this is going.)

*Answer Key:*

Yes, you guessed it. There is no correct answer, just choices that Michelle could make.

## Choice A: Flying Solo at a Wedding

After much deliberation, Michelle decides to be faithful to her history with Cathy and to fly cross-country, at great expense, for the rehearsal dinner, an extravagant wedding, and a Sunday brunch. She catches a red-eye Thursday night and arrives in New York on Friday morning, groggy and alone. The day is hers, but she has to be at a last-minute fitting for her bridesmaid's dress at one P.M. (because she lives in California, she could do this no earlier). There she meets the rest of the bridesmaid party—the gang of nine. And while she cannot muster the excitement and giddiness they seem to emit, she does at least take solace in the fact that one of them is, like her, flying solo for the weekend.

The rehearsal dinner is Michelle's first signal that she might in for a rough weekend. Is there anything more annoying than being among the handful of single people in a room full of married couples? Cathy's soon-to-be-betrothed is a real estate developer, and most of his friends are in the same business. As an architect, Michelle deals with people like this every day and has little use for their profiteering priorities and their lack of appreciation of her subtle artfulness. Being forced to make nice with them at a wedding is more than she can tolerate, so she turns to the house wine that's being poured so liberally. This suits her well until the speech-giving portion of the evening begins. Michelle and the other eight bridesmaids stumble through a rendition of "The

Age of Aquarius," rewritten to reflect the story of the bride and groom. Michelle, for her part, keeps to the side and mouths the words, returning swiftly to her seat. The evening ends and she returns to her hotel room, feeling more alone than she has in some time. She laughs at the silliness of the affair, vowing to elope if and when she finds a husband.

Michelle is awakened early Saturday by the sound of a garbage truck rumbling down the street. Though the wedding ceremony is not scheduled to begin until six-thirty that evening, being a bridesmaid is an all-day affair. Hair. Makeup. General cavorting and telling the bride how gorgeous she looks. Then pictures. And then second takes. And the candid shots. She feels as though she's playing a bit part in someone else's movie—an accessory flown in from the West Coast to make it look as though the bride has a lot of friends. And all the small talk with Cathy's family and her in-laws. "Oh, yes, we certainly were crazy in college." "That boyfriend? Well, actually, we split up years ago." If she had someone to share this with, it might actually be comical. As it stands, Michelle can't wait until the reception starts and she returns to her life as a civilian with open bar privileges.

Yet amid all the despair and taffeta, Michelle has been given a glimmer of hope. The sole single male (discounting the groom's twenty-two-year-old brother) has been briefed about Michelle and is excited to meet her. "Nigel," Cathy says, in between photos. Nigel is the groom's English friend from his junior year abroad. "He works in advertising," Cathy continues. "You know, he's creative, like you. You guys are going to hit it off." So, as the wedding party makes its way down the aisle, Michelle finds herself scanning the groom's side, looking for a creative-looking Englishman.

As it turns out, Nigel is Welsh. Moreover, his "creative" job in advertising involves stuffing coupons into mass mailers that are sent out to anybody who has ever used a credit card. But he does have a cute accent, and he even claims to have once seen Joy Division at the Hacienda, in Manchester, England. So, while Nigel is probably not the man Michelle will marry, he's clever enough to be a drinking and dancing companion for the evening.

As the weekend ends, Michelle realizes that she should probably have stuck to her guns and declined the invitation. It was not the annoyance of being single at a couple's events, or even Nigel's drunken efforts to seduce her. Rather, she realized that she and Cathy have nothing in common, and it's not worth putting herself into situations where she has to feign interest or emotion.

## Choice B: Stuck in New York with the Bad Date Blues Again

Good old Paul. Mr. Middle of the Road. He has a good job, went to a good school, and aspires to the good life. He is not lazy but he doesn't work too hard. He likes what he likes, and he's not that interested in expanding his worldview. Sure, he goes with Michelle to museums and galleries, but he never seems to have much fun. And she knows he's just someone she is dating for now, until the real thing comes along. They've been seeing each other for two months. And she has a dilemma. A friend from college is getting married, and she's been invited with a date.

If Paul were someone she really liked, she'd be nervous that inviting him to a wedding at such an early juncture might seem too "serious." In this case, she doesn't really care what he thinks. She's really just trying to figure out which case is worst: going solo, or going with Paul. Going solo is no fun, but can she stand him for three days? He is good in bed, and three evenings in a hotel room could be fun. But what about all that daylight time? And introducing him to people at the wedding and having to use the same disclaimer: "He's *not* my boyfriend, we're just . . . friends."

In the end, Paul gets the nod. He was sweet, even "boy-friendly" when she invited him, feigning excitement and suggesting that he would be delighted to escort her to such an important affair. For a brief moment, she thought she might be able to like him. But then he reverted to his Beavis and Butt-Headlike self and the sensation passed. Thankfully, Michelle's role as a brides-maid would distract her from having to deal with him too much—or so she thought.

Checking into the hotel, Michelle realizes for the first time that she has committed to spending three days with a guy she can hardly sit next to during a three-hour movie. And the trip itself has too many hallmarks of seriousness, from the concierge mistaking them for being married to the "his and her" bathrobes laid out on the king-size bed. Rather than serving as a fuck buddy and dinner date, Paul has become an unwitting reminder to Michelle of everything she does not have in her life.

The actual wedding only makes matters worse. By the time the bride and groom had their first dance, Michelle could hardly even look at Paul. Of course, she knew he hadn't done anything wrong. He was simply a stand-in, along for the ride. She should have known better than to hope an in-between guy could some-how turn into her full-time man.

## Choice C: The Rules of Engagement

Cathy's wedding presents Michelle with the perfect opportunity to put in motion a plan that sounds like the plot of a soon-to-be-released Kate Hudson movie (or perhaps a fantasy that a lot of single women have in the backs of their minds): Fly to New York, head to a bar, and find a man to play along with the ruse that they are engaged and attend the wedding weekend with her, as her fiancé. The plan was hatched during a ski weekend in Lake Tahoe by Michelle and a group of her single girlfriends. None of them has had the guts, however, to see it through. Michelle would be the first and, in doing so, she'd win a pretty nice prize: the spa treatment of her choice, plus a new pair of skis. Because she had not seen Cathy or any of her friends in a few years, it would seem plausible. And where better to find a coconspirator than New York City? If she had the gumption to follow through, this just might work, she thought as she plotted the caper thirty thousand feet over Missouri on a Thursday afternoon.

New York, New York. It's a helluva town, and one filled with eligible single men who might have their entire weekend free and want to commit a wedding-based fraud. Well, in a city of eight million, there had to be one man willing to help her live out a dream. As it turned out, there were several. In fact, Michelle found a number of willing suitors at the first bar she walked into (a famous old joint in the West Village known for its burgers and bartenders). And in order to select the right man for the job, she set up a series of tests, mainly to determine how well the men could act (or, really, lie) under pressure and the influence of alcohol.

The man she picks, Thomas, is a thirty-six-year-old business development executive for an Internet company (yes, they still exist) who was a drama minor at Yale. He is good-looking, with sandy brown hair and a charming demeanor. Were Michelle to meet him on a blind date, she'd be pleased. This is a good thing because, essentially, they are committing to a three-day-long blind engagement. They spend a few hours getting their story straight and agree to meet at five P.M. the next day, before the rehearsal dinner.

Freed of the bounds of mundane reality, they build a fantasy relationship. Michelle would dazzle her college friends with the tale of her engagement, which began in Paris, continued in San Francisco, and culminated on a beach in Big Sur. To make matters even better, Thomas had an extra engagement ring. He had planned to give it to his last girlfriend, before she ran off with someone else (lucky for Michelle it was a classic diamond solitaire in a Tiffany setting). Now their ruse was complete. It was simply a matter of execution.

"You're engaged!!" screams Missy Gordon, one of the many college friends Michelle lost track of when she moved to San Francisco, before Michelle can even walk in the door of the Italian restaurant where the rehearsal dinner is being held. And that is how the rest of the evening goes, with Michelle nearly stealing the thunder from the actual bride and groom. She even gives a funny impromptu speech, with a special shout-out to her man, Thomas, the light of her life.

As they left the restaurant, Michelle invites Thomas to stay the night in her hotel. "It's committing to the role," she says in-nocently, holding his hand as they walk along Fifty-ninth Street, the southern border of Central Park. Thomas, ever the actor, abides, and they return to their room for a sleepless evening of premarital fun.

The next morning, Michelle has forgotten all about the wed-ding and her bridesmaid responsibilities. And though she has only known the man next to her in bed for a day, she feels oddly comfortable. She should have tried this years ago. It certainly beats the dismal dating treadmill and all those guys she knew she was not that into. Fake engagement beats real life any day of the week.

Thomas sat by himself during the ceremony but Michelle caught a glimpse of him, clad in his tuxedo, as she walked down the aisle. She smiled at her "fiancé," excited to share pigs in a blanket with him at the reception. Was she really into this guy or was it just the excitement of her scheme that had her floating along in her satin Stuart Weitzman pumps (which, because they were dyed to match her teal blue dress, she would wear exactly once)?

As far as dates go, Thomas was a dream. He pushed Michelle's chair in when she sat down at the table (they were seated with a nice group of other couples, not at the misfit singles table), and he was an excellent dancer (the overdone six-piece band was an-other story). And more than anything, having him there allowed her to avoid the gaze and the questions of the others at the wed-ding, the "why aren't you married" line of inquiry that, even if unspoken, is always present. She was playing the role, and the charade had confirmed that she could be an equal member in a healthy relationship.

In the end, Michelle decides that while the experience was exhilarating, it'll never work with Thomas. Her willing coconspirator sadly agreed, and they said good-bye. On the plane back to San Francisco, Michelle feels elated. She knows now that finding a man is possible, she just needs to look in a different way, and see with new eyes.

part 3 **THE CYCLE**

*"I like a man who can run faster than I can."*

—*Gentleman Prefer Blondes*

*A*h, the dating life. It seems so exciting in theory. Meeting up for designer martinis at trendy bars and laughing about life, work, the future, the world, with hopes of everlasting love and cosmic alignment. And sometimes it feels like you're really clicking, at least for a few moments, and you think, *Wow, maybe this guy will be "the one."*

Of course, more often than not, the evening ends up a disappointment. Sure, you didn't like him, but you become plagued with doubt—Should I have kissed him or not? Will he call me or not?—nearly forgetting the most important question of all: Did you like him *or not?*

Perhaps it was only a first date. Perhaps things

seemed to be going okay before you caught him eyeing another woman at the bar or talking about his last girlfriend in romantic or vitriolic terms. Or maybe he began lecturing you about his very important job, speaking to you without a trace of irony about his ambitions to take over corporate America one Power Point slide at a time. And ultimately when you return home alone again, you come to the sorry conclusion that he's not the one after all.

That is, until he calls you a few days later and asks you out again, and you think, *Wow, maybe he liked me. Well, I guess he wasn't so bad really. Hey, you never know.*

Welcome to the wonderful world of meantime romance.

Sound familiar?

You're not alone. In fact, there are about twenty-eight million single women in the United States who go through this exact scenario time and time again. You're trapped on the dismal dating treadmill and, like George Jetson in the classic cartoon, you can't get off the crazy thing. But the difference is that treadmills serve a purpose: They keep you fit. Sadly, when it comes to dating, the only muscles you exercise is your ability to feign interest in someone you basically wouldn't like enough to have lunch with—that is, if they happened to be someone you met at a party or work and they were, instead, a woman. So the question remains, how do you get off that dating treadmill without falling flat on your face? How do you take that first decisive step and say, "No, he wasn't the one. And even if he does like me and I'm not seeing anyone else, I don't like him enough to give him the time of day, let alone most of my night."

## Are You a Victim of the Industrial-Dating Complex?

*"Match.com, Nerve.com, HurryDate, Jdate—I'm not even
Jewish but I figure it's easier to convert than to meet a good
guy—I've tried them all, and I'm so fed up. From writing
the profiles to strategizing the photo, to answering twenty-
seven e-mails a day, not to mention the dates themselves,
it's a full-time job. I'm a manager in the office; I don't want
to have to use spreadsheets to run my dating life."*

—Jennifer, 29, public relations executive, New York

With the proliferation of online dating services over the past five
years, the dismal dating treadmill has hit hyperspeed. Why? Because, from a pure numbers perspective, single people are able
to quasi-connect with one another more quickly, and more im-
personally, than ever before. In the online dating world, you can
meet ten guys an hour, if you're so inclined.

Will you learn about their deeper spiritual qualities? No. Can
you be certain that the picture they sent is even accurate to this
decade? No. But in terms of pure transactional ability, online
dating is an efficient and frictionless means of working the numbers in your favor: more possibilities, less time and effort.

But does efficiency make dating easier or does it just serve to
further perpetuate the endless cycle of settling? In many ways,
online dating is an expression of a high-tech culture that wants
quick fixes and instant gratification. It's the eBay of dating. If the
offering is decent, you might as well hedge your bets and put in a
low bid. Online dating turns love into a packaged commodity,
one mouse click away.

Of course, some online dating services have grown more attuned to the deeper nuances of interpersonal "chemistry," or so they say. With "scientific matching technologies" and "proprietary relationship engines," finding a boyfriend is now as easy as buying the new Eminem CD on Amazon.com. But can you really fall in love with someone's answer sheet on a multiple-choice questionnaire? In an ideal world, isn't physical, emotional, and sexual attraction based on a wonderfully mysterious synergy of unconscious impulses we can't even fathom ourselves?

Each day there seem to be more and more ways to find love quickly, from online dating services to speed-dating to singles events geared toward meeting as many possible candidates for lifetime partnership in as short a time frame as possible (complete with index cards and pencils in case you forget your future mate's name). And that gets you right back on that treadmill, dating for dating's sake.

In our noisy interconnected world, it's easier to go on a date than to bear the loneliness of another night at home. And even when you're home, how many hours do you spend surfing through online dating sites, reading relationship columns or blogs, literally or metaphorically shopping for relationships with men who, more than likely, you wouldn't be that into anyway?

The odious roots of the industrial-dating complex extend beyond the Internet and speed-dating marathons. From guidebooks to talk shows to magazines, everyone claims to have an answer to the eternal conundrum. Maybe it's which aisle in the supermarket to shop in. Maybe it's whether or not to call. Maybe it's using the wisdom of the "program" (applying the lessons of a Harvard MBA to finding a man). Hey, maybe you should try the Kabbalah (it worked for Madonna). And what is the booby prize at the end of this treasure hunt? You might have guessed it already but apparently "he's just not that into you."

Anyone, and everyone, seems to have *the* answer. And yes, we might as well say it: What about this book? Isn't that why you bought it in the first place? But if I manage to get one point across at all, please let it be this one: Trust yourself. Trust your instincts. Don't get wrapped up in finding or keeping a man, resorting to rules and tactics and playing the numbers game. Learn to stop succumbing to the pressure to achieve coupledom. That way, when the real thing comes along, you will be ready, willing, and able to jump in with both feet, not caught on some infernal treadmill where you wouldn't know the real thing if it slapped you in the fanny pack.

## Dating at the Speed of Light

> *"I don't have time to spend three weeks getting to know a guy. If I don't feel it within the first five minutes, why would I waste the effort?"*
>
> —Naomi, 31, fashion designer, New York

Faster. Bigger. Better. That is the mantra of the digital age. We're in a rush to get to the next big thing—so much so that we never have time to appreciate what came before it. The next big thing is better simply because it's newer. The same logic defines dating, and it's what gives rise to the treadmill effect.

In the high-speed wireless world, where daters have the potential to meet as many new people each week as they desire, individuals become devalued because there is always a new date in the queue. And let's face it, even when you're on a date, in the good, old-fashioned sense of the word, how much of a chance do you give the guy (or, conversely, how much of a chance are you given)? Is it not enough? Is it too much? Is it based on your gut feelings or his level of interest (or lack thereof)?

We have to learn how to trust our core instincts and abilities to make sound judgments. Maybe it's to give a "maybe guy" a second chance. Or maybe it's to give a "no way guy" the boot. Either way, the important thing is to listen carefully to your own instincts rather than let someone else dictate whether to pursue a relationship or even a second or third date for that matter, based on whether or not *he* happens to call or who else is on the immediate horizon.

## THE COMMON SYMPTOMS OF DATING FATIGUE

- You used to spend at least an hour getting ready for a date, and now you don't even bother with deodorant.
- You keep a cheat sheet with the names of various dates so you can keep track.
- You own a BlackBerry devoted solely to checking e-mails from online dating services.
- You've created a two-page interview form used to prescreen potential dates.
- You keep three extra outfits at work so you'll always be ready for a spur-of-the-moment date.

## Stop Me Before I Date Again

> *"I wish that I lived in Bangladesh or someplace where they have arranged marriages. My parents would just arrange the whole thing, and all I had to do was show up. An arranged marriage means never having to date and sometimes that seems more appealing."*
>
> —Susan, 38, doctor, Portland (Oregon)

Most of us couldn't imagine getting married without romance and passion. Those are the most important elements. But in historical terms, that's a rather contemporary idea. It's worth remembering that the notion of choosing a spouse purely on the basis of romantic love or physical attraction is a relatively new concept. The ancient Greeks distinguished between ten different types of love, with passionate love falling under the category of *mania,* which was actually considered unhealthy.

And "mania" is probably the right word for that flurry of excitement you feel at the hope of a budding romance (based on an online questionnaire). The dating treadmill is enough to drive you crazy. And at times, perhaps some of your behaviors do wind up bordering on clinical psychosis (doing the same thing over and over and expecting a different outcome). If you're on the treadmill, chances are you're repeating the same patterns and doing the same things over and over again. Different guy, same setting (a bar or a restaurant), and same result. (Best friend: "So, did you like him?" You: "I dunno.") What can you do? Well, you can change your habits to try and break the cycle. Clearly, what you've been doing isn't working. Isn't it time you tried something new?

The purpose of this book is *not* to give you a rote set of tactics to meet more men, such as "take a ceramics class" or "spend more time at the local basketball courts." What I'm suggesting is that you take some time to think about your own life.

Like I said in the last chapter, women's standards have gone up over the last few decades, and you've put a lot of energy into developing your own interests, passions, and goals. Now's not the time to start following the pack because the pack is simply running in circles on that silly treadmill.

## Give That Man a Makeover

> *"When I meet a guy, I don't see the man in front of me, I see the man after I've taken him shopping and redecorated his apartment. It sounds crass but guys can be molded."*
>
> —Laura, 33, music executive, Los Angeles

So, what about a fixer-upper? I suppose one way of getting off the treadmill is to settle for that guy you've been dating under the guise that you can renovate him into what you really want. Like the old paneled den your parents converted into a brand-new entertainment center after you left for college, some women think remaking a man is simply a matter of time, effort, and finding the right products. Is the boyfriend you have not doing it for you? Perhaps a new haircut and a pair of Prada loafers will do the trick. Well, there's also the matter of his job, but you can always work on that after you spruce up his look.

And while this may sound pretty extreme, it's a sentiment I hear surprisingly often. The truth is, we all want to change aspects of the people we date. That's our natural instinct and, in fact, somewhat healthy in moderation (don't you hate that word?). Helping your guy choose more fashionable ties and new carpeting for his bedroom can even be fun, but if you're looking to do an extreme makeover on him, you may not be suited for each other, at least not as lifetime partners.

The things that you're "not that into" about him are probably deeper than the pleated Dockers he refuses to give up. As we'll see, the dating treadmill can make you a little crazy. And if you're at the point where you're trying to turn an off-the-rack guy into a tailor-made man, you might be heading to the point of madness.

## The Mind of the Single Woman

> *"The cycle becomes so intense that I don't know when to stop and actually get to know someone. And if you do take that risk and you're wrong, you have to start all over again and get used to the treadmill."*
>
> —Marisa, 29, arts administrator, New York

The dating treadmill is more than the endless litany of bad first dates and blind setups that go awry. It's not that they aren't distressing in their own right. They are, and they do take a toll. But it's the impact that the cycle has on your dating decisions altogether that stirs my concern.

Many of the women I counsel are confused about what to do at various "milestone" points in a relationship. They begin dating someone they're unsure about simply because they're on that treadmill and forget to notice they're not getting what or *who* they want. But even as they're dating this person, they're still feeling like there's someone else better out there, if only they could get off that damned machine and get back out there in the world and look.

Others fear they'll get out of shape if they forego the treadmill. "It's like working out," says one young woman. "If you stop for a while, that makes it that much harder to start back up again ten pounds later." So, simply for the sake of keeping in shape, they stay on.

Of course, there are some women who do enjoy dating just for the sake of dating. And let me say one thing very clearly: Going on first dates can be healthy and good for you, provided you don't get swept up in the momentum of whether "he likes you." Meeting men, even if they ultimately turn out to be the wrong men, can help you decide what you really want, so there is definitely real value in it.

And, oh, yes, there is that sex thing too. If you can have sex like a man, at least sometimes, dating some less-than-ideal someone who will never, ever be "the one" can be good for the body and soul, so long as you know where to draw the line. Again, it's more a matter of being aware of yourself and your needs than following a prescribed set of rules. If you're dating a lot and can handle it, fine. If you're having casual sex and can handle it, fine too. But if the treadmill is forcing you to lower your standards, it's time to figure out an exit strategy. It may mean fewer dates in the short term, and more time with the Bunny and less time smooching between the sheets, but it'll help you finish the marathon much happier and in a far better place.

## WHAT COLOR IS YOUR LOVE PARACHUTE?

In his book *Colours of Love*, psychologist John Alan Lee condenses the Greeks' ten categories of love into six. We've listed them here, with matching "dater profiles" so that you have a handy list.

**Eros**—the most sexual and erotic of the group. These daters love the treadmill and their sexual empowerment, but they're mainly in it for the thrill of the conquest. Sure, he may be good in bed, but you probably won't see him at the breakfast table.

**Mania**—passionate love, which often includes an unhealthy dose of irrationality and possessiveness. Can you say "restraining order"? No, it's not that bad, but this guy may proclaim his love while reading you poetry on the third date, only to later declare you his property.

**Ludus**—which is Latin for "game." These guys are the game players, unserious, and they don't like to commit. Don't hate the playa, hate the game, he says. Really? Why can't you dislike both? This type of guy will wind you up just to watch you spin.

**Storge**—a brotherly or sisterly type of love, a sense of companionship. But more in the head than the heart. Oh, you're my best friend! But sometimes you want something a little more, um, physical. Come on, man, free your mind and my booty will follow.

**Agape**—kind, gentle, self-sacrificing, having a sense of duty, atrustic. He might be the best of the bunch, if he weren't always out protesting the global economy or running down to the health-food store for tofu burgers.

**Pragma**—just that, pragmatic. Based on compatibility and commonality but not chemistry; this is the love of online dating search engines. He's nice enough, and you both seem to like the same things, but something seems too predictable when you spend time together.

## The Flip Side: The Dating Sabbatical

> *"We are the puzzle pieces who seldom fit with other puzzle pieces. Romantics, idealists, eccentrics, we inhabit singledom as our natural resting state. In a world where proms and marriage define the social order, we are, by force of our personalities and inner strength, rebels."*
>
> —Sasha Cagen, founder, Quirky Alone

The organization founded by the woman quoted above seeks to destigmatize being single and exhorts singles to "resist the tyranny of coupledom." Tyranny? That's a little dramatic. But while the mission sounds almost militant, their fervor is admirable. At least they're not passively accepting singlehood or dating for the sake of dating. Quirky Alone doesn't want to step off the dating treadmill, it wants to banish it altogether.

Your view need not be as extreme but perhaps you've felt something similar at certain moments. Maybe you've wanted to step off the treadmill but you don't for fear that you'll miss an opportunity or forget how to date. But slowing things down may be a good idea.

First ask yourself: Is your desire to take a sabbatical motivated by healthy skepticism or have you just given up? If it's the latter, you're simply going from one extreme (the high-speed treadmill) to another (cementing your feet to the ground).

## Be Honest

You're running as fast as you can but you never seem to get anywhere. You're stuck in the same place, and all your evenings have an eerily similar feel. Same conversation, same recasting of your life story, but his face looks a little different in the light of the bar-of-the-moment's candlelight. If that sounds like you, then you're probably on a dating treadmill.

Help! You've dated and you can't get up (or off). Hmmm. Perhaps you've been visiting one too many online dating sites. Maybe you need to think about what you want, not whether what's-his-name from Tuesday night is going to call. Sure, the treadmill can be fun at times—after all, it moves fast and it mimics the real thing—but you're running the wrong race.

## Raise (Your Standards) and Reach (for Love)

- **You don't live online:** Online dating and all the other high-speed resources can be great, but that does not mean they should be a substitute for getting out there and living your life, with or without a man at your side.

- **Slow it down:** Hey, speed racer, there is no need to go on six dates a week. And you don't need to "know" if he's the right guy before the appetizers arrive. Give it— and him—some time. On the flip side, if you do know he's the wrong guy: Just say no! Sure, you may be flattered that he called you for a second or third date but you didn't like him to begin with. Have some faith in your ability to attract someone you actually like!

- **Making him over won't make you happy:** The guy you're dating isn't a fixer-upper, and the emperor won't change just because he has new clothes.

- **Take a break:** If you're really tired of the treadmill, it's okay to slow it down or even get off for a while.

## 10. YOU'RE NOT THAT INTO HIM EITHER, BUT YOU NEEDED HIM TO BE INTO YOU

*"Every exit is an entry somewhere else."*

—Tom Stoppard

Spend enough time on the dismal dating treadmill and you're sure to be run a little ragged. The scenery looks the same: You're speeding fast and getting nowhere. And after a while, nothing can take you by surprise, except, perhaps, your own ego.

Mark Twain once wrote, "There are no grades of vanity, there are only grades of ability in concealing it." And very often, when you date a guy you're not that into, it's your vanity and ego at work and not your heart.

It could happen in any number of ways. Maybe you slept with him; maybe he was your in-the-meantime man; maybe your friends told you to give him a chance. Or perhaps you didn't even think about him until he didn't call when he said he would. For whatever reason, you dated him because somehow dating him made you feel better about yourself. Or worse, maybe it became of the utmost importance for him to like you, regardless of cost or outcome. In short, your ego got the best of you.

## The Thrill of Being Chased

> *"I don't have to be that into a guy to like the attention he gives me."*
>
> —Stacey, 29, interior designer, Miami

Where there's a will, there's a way, and the guy you're not into probably knows this. He's scrappy and takes a street-fighting approach to dating. Sure, he may not be the best-looking guy on the block but what he lacks in looks he makes up for in persistence.

He chased you and wouldn't take no for an answer. And truth be told, it was flattering to hear him constantly say how hot you were. He was never your top choice; he was never really the one. You could take him or leave him, but slowly, over time, he wore you down. And now you're dating him, though you're still not that into him. The difference is that now, since the chase is over, he's no longer as flattering or complimentary. You got into it for your ego and now that it's not being stroked (though, to his credit, other things probably are), you're still in this less-than-satisfying relationship. But does that make you a horrible person? Like everyone else, you want to be wanted. But is your desire to be desired outweighing your ability to make good, clear choices about the men you date?

## I Wasn't That into Him *Until* He Wasn't That Into Me

> *"It doesn't matter if I'm not into the guy, I need him to be*
> *into me. Even if I don't want him to call, I still expect him*
> *to. If he doesn't, it's like, What's wrong with me? Some-*
> *times it hurts even more when you're not into him because*
> *then you must really be a loser."*
>
> —Kim, 33, sales manager, Denver

The second time you agreed to go out with him, you did so with reluctance. I mean, the first date wasn't all bad, but it wasn't that good either. You weren't even planning to return his call but, hell, you were feeling kind of down. A dinner with someone who actually appeared to be into you seemed like a nice change of pace— especially after your last boyfriend. But even as you said yes, you started thinking of excuses for turning down the next date.

And then it happened. After the second or maybe even third date, he didn't call or e-mail. After several days passed, he began to occupy more of your mind (or, rather, his inaction did). You dialed his work number a few times but hung up before he could answer. And five days after the last date, you finally broke down and sent him an e-mail. He never replied.

This is where the intense overanalysis begins: Did he receive your e-mail? Was he away on a business trip? Was his server down or was he in meetings all day? Some books might tell you he's just not that into you. But you shouldn't really care about what his passive behavior suggests because the truth of the matter is you were never that into him to begin with—that is, until he acted like he was not that into you.

Then you became very, *very* interested. Or your ego became interested in the validation. You didn't want him, but you wanted him to want you. You wondered why the change, had you been less attractive this last go-round? Did you have a bit of salad stuck between your teeth during dinner? Was the outfit you picked for its ability to hide that PMS bloating not that flattering after all? Did he meet someone else he liked more? Suddenly, it's the challenge of making him want you that becomes the motivating factor.

This, clearly, is no way to secure a happy and loving relationship but it happens all the time. And I mean all the time. So, be honest. Haven't you been in this situation before? You go on a date with a guy you're not particularly attracted to simply for a little harmless ego boost. And that somehow turns into a second date or maybe even a third one. And the dating is still fun. Harmless and reassuring, right? Not really. That's followed by waiting for the e-mail or phone call that, for some reason, just doesn't come. Suddenly, you're completely obsessed, hook, line, and stinker.

A subtle variation on the situation above is the even more odious "pullback." This occurs when a guy comes on really strong and is very persistent right until he reels you in (which often involves giving up a little somethin' somethin' along the way). Then he suddenly pulls back. It's as base and manipulative as picking teams for a school-yard game of kickball, but you know what, folks? It works (almost) every time.

## WHY MEN CHASE AND RETREAT

In fishing it's called the "catch and release." Your guy spends all his time and energy getting you into the boat and, once you're there, he throws you overboard. Why do men do this? Many reasons. Partially, it's his ego at work (just like yours is when you want to be chased). It's sort of reenacting a cartoonlike charade over and over again (repetition compulsion, as Freud called it). In lay terms (pardon the pun), it's like Popeye chasing Olive Oyl until he finally grasps her in his arms as the final music drones, only there's no foil (remember Brutus?), so he pulls back instead. As simple as TV and other dating books make men out to be, we're actually driven by motivations that run deeper than sex, sports, and beer. But back to your guy for a moment: For him, the catch is the ego gratification he needs, and the release is his way of letting you go before you do the same to him. Now, this does not mean that he wasn't interested in the sex too. If you had slept with him, then he may have gotten all he was interested in getting, and his pulling back was a form of fleeing.

It's also possible that he pulled back for the "right" reasons. That is, he might have liked you but rightly sensed your misgivings. Or maybe he didn't want to push too hard. The only way to know is to communicate, and too often in the dating world you're dealing with crossed signals and mixed messages.

## The Duckling Became a Swan

> *"It's the more plain-looking guys that get you every time."*
>
> —Claudia, 33, sales, Cleveland

All the dating books recommend avoiding the good-looking guys at all costs because they'll never commit, and if they do, they're more likely to cheat. Hmmm. Has that been true in your experience? Maybe, but you've got to look out for some of those ugly ducklings too. Some of them are schemers just like their more handsome brethren. It goes back to that old adage that you can't judge a book by its cover. These less-than-pretty boys know an attractive woman can fall for an unattractive guy. Funny thing is that guys are much pickier about looks because they can't get past the visual. Women are picky too but they take the whole picture into consideration. Sometimes an ugly duckling has a great sense of humor, a cute smile, or nice eyes. And like magic, he transforms into a beautiful swan right before your very eyes.

But then as soon you begin to see him as attractive, without warning, he pulls the rug out from under you, and you're devastated. Your friends can't believe you're hung up on him because they never saw the swan, just the ugly duckling. And even as you laugh with your friends over margaritas about your latest humiliation and say, "I can't believe that little grease monkey blew me off," the truth is, it still hurts.

## The Fall Is the Hardest Part

*"I don't even know how it happened. One minute I wasn't even interested, and the next I find myself unable to do anything but think of him."*

—Nicole, 32, architect, Chicago

George Sand wrote, "Vanity is the quicksand of reason," and when you're lowering your standards, you're sometimes just inches away from stepping in a whole big mess of the stuff.

But how do you know if it's just a bruised ego or genuine feelings? How do you know if you really like him? It's time for me to put on my clinical hat for a moment and ask you a few questions about Mr. I Can't Believe He's Not into *Me*:

*Is he taking on special meaning?* Once we start liking someone, we begin to see that person's unique qualities. Sure, he started out as just another spin on the dating treadmill but now the others start to pale compared to him. There's something, well, different about him. He's funnier, more intelligent, more sensitive than the rest of them. In short, he's becoming special to you.

*Is he commanding more of your attention?* When we start to like someone, we spend a lot more time thinking about that person. We start to neglect family, friends, and work. You check your answering machine, you wait for his e-mails, you wonder if something's wrong with AOL. You find yourself thinking more and more about your times together, the little details like what he ordered to drink and the color of the shirt he wore on your last date. Random things and odd events start to remind you of him. Yup, it's true. He's got your attention.

*Are you wearing rose-colored glasses?* When we like someone, we tend to aggrandize them, to make a lot out of the little things, to push aside their faults and to even see those faults as being cute or funny. We see their good qualities through a magnifying glass. Our friends often don't get what we see in that person but it doesn't matter because we do. Ask yourself: Are you seeing this guy in a way that makes your friends think you've swallowed a batch of hallucinogens? If so, it's time to get a new pair of glasses.

*Do you feel consumed by emotion?* Are you passionate about him? Have you started and then stopped yourself from sending him little e-mails? When you're with him, do those emotions intensify? Do you have to work hard to seem calm and collected when your mind is racing? Are you experiencing mood swings, from happiness to sadness, many of which are dependent on the attention you're getting or not getting from him?

*Are you eating? Are you sleeping?* Often when we start to like someone, we feel a sense of exhilaration, a tremendous sense of energy. Our hearts race, and we forget to eat and have trouble sleeping.

*Are you changing yourself?* Whether it's your clothes, your hair, your taste in music and movies, or even your priorities and values, when we start to like someone, we often emulate them and change ourselves in ways that we think will make us more appealing and attractive to that person.

*Do you want exclusivity from him?* If he was just a fuck buddy, it shouldn't matter if he sleeps with other women. When we don't really like someone, we don't care if they see other people. It's only when we start to like someone that we want or even demand exclusivity.

## ADDICTED TO LOVE

If it helps, you can think of the sensation of falling for somebody (even someone you thought you weren't that into) as the process of addiction, and I mean that literally. "Because romantic love is such a euphoric 'high,' because this passion is exceedingly difficult to control, and because it produces craving, obsession, compulsion, distortion of reality, emotional and physical dependence, personality change, and loss of self-control, many psychologists regard romantic love as an addiction—a positive addiction when your love is returned, a horribly negative fixation when your love is spurned and you can't let go." Those are the words of Helen Fisher, a noted anthropologist.

The situation started off harmlessly enough. A few dates, not that big a deal—you didn't even like the guy. But then you got a little lonely, or you liked having your ego (and lower parts) stroked and you invested yourself in the process a little more. And somewhere along the line, you became a full-fledged junkie, jonesing for your next fix. Like all "drugs of abuse," love affects a single pathway in the brain (the mesolimbic reward system) that is activated by that old dopamine. When neuroscientists compared the brain scans of their love-stricken subjects with those of men and women who had injected cocaine or opioids, they found that many of the same brain regions became active.

So, how can you free yourself from something so addictive? I have two words for you: cold turkey. Like any addiction, giving up the guy will be difficult at first. You'll be tempted to backslide by a late-night phone call or a sappy song that reminds you of the way you were. But over time your resilience will improve, and in a matter of months you'll look back and wonder what the big fuss was all about. You'll realize just how much you were not that into him, and your addiction will seem like a distant memory.

---

If you answered yes to some or all of these questions, you're not just starting to like that person, you're starting to love that person. Yes, you're falling, and you might be on your way to falling really hard. It doesn't matter how you got to this place, whether it started out as just sex, or he was "in the meantime," or just a run on the dating treadmill—once you start loving someone, all bets are off.

But if these feelings are reciprocated, then you're off on the roller coaster of romance. Chances are, though, that if that were the case, you probably wouldn't be reading this book.

So what does it mean if your feelings aren't reciprocated? Well, you're probably going to be taken for a ride, one that includes painful feelings of rejection, anger, jealousy, paranoia, and ultimately resignation. In some ways the process is chemically driven (our old friend dopamine again, as well as some others), and it's ironic that the same chemicals that enable us to experience the joys and ecstasies of romantic love can also lead us to the bowels of despair.

## The Flip Side: You're *Only* Into Guys You're Not Really Into

> "I tend to find myself in relationships with men I know I'm not that into because it's safer."
>
> —Olivia, 31, advertising sales, Atlanta

One of the possible scenarios of falling for a man who you were never that into to begin with, or who reeled you in simply for the challenge, is that it may be a relationship in which the main attraction is simply the lack of attraction. Strange as that may sound, it happens a lot.

A lot of women end up dating men who they know they're not into (or who are otherwise inappropriate for them) because there is less risk if it doesn't work out. When it ends, they can say, "Well, he was not right for me anyway," and then climb right back onto that treadmill, only to repeat the cycle.

The problem with this sort of pattern is that it eventually results in dramatically lowered standards. You may think you're giving up a little, but as a result, you end up giving up a whole lot.

And how much worse is it when the loser guy you went out with primarily as an ego boost (let's be honest here) winds up rejecting you? How much worse do you feel as a result? It's a vicious downward spiral that you originally got into for the presumed safety of superiority, and you then end up feeling lower than low in the end. I mean, how could this not-so-attractive guy who doesn't dress particularly well and still lives with his mother wind up rejecting *you?* Could he really have found someone better? Is the dating scene truly this cutthroat?

And, if so, what will you do about it? The next time, you'll probably aim even lower. And so it continues until you hit rock bottom and finally decide that you're better off alone.

## Be Honest

You were not that into him but, somewhere along the line, your ego got involved, and then you needed him to be into you. Perhaps you just wanted the attention and were then baffled when he pulled away. Or maybe you became so into making him like you that you got into a relationship just so you could validate yourself. But what happened next? Well, maybe it went nowhere, and you were back on the dismal dating cycle.

Or, perhaps for better or worse, you actually started to like him and found yourself falling for him. If the feelings were reciprocated, and there turned out to be more to this guy than initially met the eye, then great, you may be on your way to something meaningful and real. But if he's everything you ever thought he wasn't and less, you're bound to feel worse for the time and energy you've spent pretending you were into him in the first place.

## Raise (Your Standards) and Reach (for Love)

- **Let go of the ego:** If you're into him just because you need him to be into you, you're letting your ego drive your decisions. And while you can never entirely remove your ego from your dating life, don't let it run (or ruin) it.

- **Don't play the game:** If you're just in it because he's chasing you, then you're playing the game as well. Instead, use good sportsmanship and have enough confidence to bow out and send him on his way.
- **After the fall:** Even if you think you're not into him, you may be falling harder than you think. Be on the lookout for the telltale signs. And if the feelings aren't being reciprocated, remind yourself about what you didn't see in him in the first place and get the hell out while the going is still good.
- **Don't play it completely safe:** If you're sticking with guys who you're not into simply because there is less at risk, you're lowering your standards. To get what you really deserve, you'll have to put something on the line.

## 11. YOU'RE NOT THAT INTO HIM (OR ANYONE), AND YOU'VE GIVEN UP ON FINDING LOVE

*"When you realize you want to spend the rest of your life with somebody, you want the rest of your life to start as soon as possible."*

—*When Harry Met Sally*

So, you've given up on love, have you? You're done with it. You've had your fill and you're washing your hands of the whole sordid affair: the empty hookups, the long string of mediocre Mr. Mean-times, the never-ending treadmill of dismal dating you called your love life. You've spent more than enough precious time and energy learning to like some jerk only to realize *he's just not that into you*. And how can anyone blame you for throwing in the towel?

You have every right to give up. In fact, I'd like to offer you my heartiest congratulations!

You did it! You made it! I wasn't sure you had it in you but you passed the test!

Let me explain: While we're in this chapter, think of me as the Willy Wonka of romance (minus the curly hair and funny hat, of course).

Way back when, you started out with a golden ticket (along with an open heart); you were ready for your trip to the Candy Factory of Love and Everlasting Happiness. But somewhere along the way, you took a wrong turn, and you were detoured. You wound up on the dismal dating treadmill and finally got rerouted.

## The Eternal Myth of Love

The golden ticket was a ruse. The truth is, everyone got one and everyone believed they were the lucky ones. It's called the myth of love: Our soul mate is out there and once we find him/her we'll live happily ever after. Isn't that how it's portrayed in the movies?

Romantic love is as old as storytelling itself, and it's one of our most honored traditions. Girl meets boy and they fall in love. Isn't that how it's supposed to work? Sort of, at least on paper. But you know better than that by now.

Sure, it has taken a while but you wised up. You don't believe in happily ever after anymore. You know the golden ticket was a sham and, at this point, you're sorry you even bothered showing up—what was supposed to be a breezy tour was actually a back-door draft into an ongoing war of anguish and woe. And at this point, you've been through so much you're a candidate for a permanent Purple Heart.

So, here you are, pissed off, defeated—and ready to leave

your Everlasting Gobstopper of Love on the table and walk away.

Well, hold on there just a minute. (This is where I get to play Willy Wonka and tell you to wait, ya know.) I just tabulated the scores and guess what? You won! (Don't worry, I'm not going to make you take a ride on my magic elevator.) I knew you were better than the rest. And just when you thought it was all over, it's just the beginning.

All those times you lowered your standards and were tempted to settle? You didn't. You may have gotten caught up, you may have gotten scared, freaked out, bummed out, but you didn't settle. You didn't give up, not completely. In fact, all the experiences you've had up to now will actually pave the way to higher standards and the type of relationship you deserve. It may not be a fairy tale but it'll be based in reality, and it'll be with someone you're really into.

While compromising may be the name of the game in the world of business, in this candy land we call love, it is *not* compromising your standards and remembering what you really want and deserve that will ultimately win the day.

## The Love Wars: A Veteran's Hall of Fame

Maybe you slept with a bunch of guys along the way, attempting to have sex like a man. Sometimes it was fun and rewarding, at least on the physical level. Other times, it was just a warm body to heat up the cold stretch of empty nights. You have needs, and you enjoy sex, and hell, you even like the *fleeting* sense of intimacy. Just don't mistake it for love—or so you think.

And while you haven't resigned yourself to a lifetime of mean-ingless sex, you've simply found ways to cope with being single in the meantime. Secretly, you are hoping that the real thing will materialize through no effort of your own and magically fall into place (without too much mess or disruption, of course). Unfor-tunately, life has a nasty habit of neutering even our best-*laid* plans. And try as we might to keep our distance, eventually our feelings seem to get involved. And that's when a lot of women (maybe you're one of them) throw in the towel and decide to go it alone.

**Meet Victoria.** A thirty-seven-year-old marketing executive, Vickie was so intent on having sex like a man that it became her regular MO. In fact, she was sort of proud of her sexual freedom, pointing to her career as a trophy earned through sacrificing emotional attachments (unlike her perpetually whiny, less suc-cessful friends). She had no time for a relationship, just a few male friends she rang up when she started feeling that infernal itch. She was convinced that she didn't need love, that she was completely immune to its lure. Deep down, however, her longing for companionship finally took its toll. At some point, she started hoping, even fantasizing, that one of her fuck buddies would transform into an actual boyfriend, a partner, just for conve-nience's sake, or so she told herself at first. After all, it made sense. They were already friends. They were sexually compatible. But then when she realized that her fuck buddies regarded her as solely a meantimer, she was just as heartbroken as the rest of us. Well, maybe just a little bit more. And that's when she decided to focus on her career and stick with her Rabbit instead.

And then there's **Monique.** A twenty-nine-year-old graphic designer, Monique always seemed to be chasing after the wrong men simply because she felt better about herself when she was wanted by a man, any man, no matter who he was. Monique suffered through a long string of meantimers, each of whom she placed on a pedestal in order to prevent herself from admitting that they were completely beneath her. But they knew the truth, and they secretly despised her for it. So one after the next, they put her down and ultimately left her, which only made her more insecure and lonely than she had been the last time. Finally, she gave up altogether. Even if she was lonelier, at least it was less painful not to go through this hideous cycle again and again.

Let's hope, though, that you're not like **Chloe.** A thirty-three-year-old teacher, Chloe married a guy she knew was not right simply because all her friends were getting married and her parents liked him. Chloe felt like she would never meet the right man and decided it wasn't worth wasting the rest of her fertile years trying. So, she took what she could get, even though she knew deep down she was settling. Still, she was happy to be able to show off an engagement ring, and she lost herself in the details of planning the wedding, so much so that before she knew it, Mr. Meantime was her husband. And that's how Chloe gave up. Yup, it's true, marry the wrong man for the wrong reason, and you might as well be home alone with the Rabbit. Only it's much, much worse, because in Chloe's situation you're never, yet always, alone.

If you are anything at all like Victoria or Monique, consider yourself lucky. Sure, you may have had your fair share of casual sex or bad relationships but at least you didn't do what Chloe did (I hope). At least you didn't sacrifice your freedom and your future for the token assurance of a ring.

So, now I'm here to tell you that you won the Willy Wonka

factory. And that means it's time to get back out there and believe in yourself and play the game for real. You may have lost before but you managed to regain your stride by refusing to settle. You've had plenty of time to reflect and recuperate. You believed in yourself enough not to settle, and now the time has come to get back out there and do it for real.

I know you probably have misgivings about winding up back on that dating treadmill. You are afraid of repeating past mistakes. You know that try as you might to have sex without feelings, chances are you *will* feel something for someone you sleep with whether or not you intend it. And you don't want to fall for the wrong guy again.

Or maybe you no longer trust your own taste in men. You know you have a tendency to look beyond a guy's faults and force yourself to fall in love with your own fabrication, which only leads to resentment and a bitter downward spiral.

But listen: You're smart enough not to have ended up like Chloe. You weren't so sad, so desperate that you allowed yourself to marry someone you knew was completely wrong for you (or maybe you're fresh off the dating "marry-go-round" and ready to do better this time). But first, you need to trust yourself. Because the truth is, you do know better. You have learned from the past. You got off the treadmill for one reason or another. And when lesser friends like Chloe settled, you persevered.

And now it's time to trust yourself again to get out and start dating again. How?

Well, if you go on a first date and realize he's not the one for you, decide then and there to cut the cord. No more game playing or getting caught up waiting to see if he'll ask you out again.

If you like him, sure, give him another chance, but if and when you know he's not the one for you, *just say no.*

Or say you decide that you're up for some casual sex (hey, we all have our needs). Still, you're afraid of becoming too attached. Easy. Don't take his number. Don't give him your number. Or simply don't return his call if he already has it. If you know in your heart of hearts that you're not that into him but that you are likely to get too emotionally attached if you sleep with him more than once, *don't do it.* Walk like a man (right out that door, without looking back).

What you're ready to give up on is the pursuit of love, at least the way you've been pursuing it, and that's scary because better to work with the devil you know than one you don't know.

But you can't go back, not after all you've been through. You're ready for a change.

And why would you want to? All along you've been reaching for the love you deserve. It's taken a long time to get to this point.

You're ready for a ride in the glass elevator (okay, I know I said no glass elevator, but the metaphor fit too well here)—as high as your standards will take you.

So pick that Gobstopper up off the table and get going. And while you're up there, take a look below at the candy factory and all the people running around with their golden tickets, doing everything you were doing (dating Mr. Meantime, running the dismal dating treadmill, and so on). From your vantage point, they all look so tiny and pathetic. You're so much bigger than that.

You're not that into him but that didn't stop you from sleeping with him; it didn't stop you from dating him; it didn't stop you from liking him. You're not that into him but you know what?

It didn't stop you.

## Be Honest

Well, you thought about it. After all those dismal dates and in-betweens and the battles you fought, you walked to the brink and were ready to toss it all away. You had nearly given up on love and almost just settled for the next guy who walked past you on the street. *Why not?* you figured. He'd probably have been no better but also no worse than any of the others. So, there you stand at the river's edge, ready to toss it all asunder.

But something happened. A voice, a realization. It came to you, the clarion call. Of course love is still out there, and of course you will find it. Will it look exactly like the made-for-TV version? No, but that's okay. It'll be better because it will be real. The first step is to get off the treadmill, which you've done (or will do soon). From there, you're simply a stroll through the candy factory away.

## Raise (Your Standards) and Reach (for Love)

- **Love is not a Hallmark card:** Real love is probably not like the thing you've been seeking your whole life. And it's not some gift-wrapped box that brings eternal happiness. But once you grasp the reality, you'll be much closer to finding it.

- **You're a proud veteran:** You're grizzled and weary from the dating war front. But don't get bitter. Be proud. All that time you've put in will pay off, as it makes you a wiser, more savvy veteran in the game of love.

- **Hark, the voice is calling:** You've heard the call, now go out and answer it. You got off the treadmill, now get off your butt and get back out there, and trust yourself this time.

- **Pick up the towel:** You threw it down when you gave up, but it's not too late to pick it back up. You're heading in a new direction and you won't have the treadmill to speed you along. This is new ground and you'll have to do all the running yourself but the finish line is much more rewarding here.

## 12. THE CAGE

*"There are only four questions of value in life, Don Octavio. What is sacred? Of what is the spirit made? What is worth living for, and what is worth dying for? The answer to each is the same: only love."*

—Don Juan De Marco

s I reread these last three chapters on the "cycle" of mental and emotional patterns that we often get stuck in, I can't help but think how much of it applies to my own experience—women aren't the only ones who often give up on finding love.

Before I met my wife, Lisa, the true love of my life, I'd been stuck in a five-year relationship with a woman to whom I was engaged, although we had never set a date for the wedding.

She was an actress/dancer, and the idea to propose

to her occurred while she was away on tour for a production of *A Chorus Line*. I should have just "kissed today good-bye" right then and moved on but, as you know, an "in-the-meantime" romance can sneak up on you and become your full-time life. So why did I go so far as to propose? Was it just a matter of time and obligation? I guess like I felt it had been five years, and I owed her that much.

But what about me? What did I owe myself? Clearly, not much. Actually, though, I wasn't even aware of it at the time. Only in retrospect did I come to realize how low my sense of self-esteem had been at the time. I hadn't given up on finding love because I never felt that I deserved it in the first place.

One school of psychology proposes that we're attracted to those who symbolize the parent with whom we're most conflicted. In my case, that would be my father. My parents separated when I was three and after the divorce, I would visit my dad on weekends at the Chelsea Hotel (a notorious Bohemian haunt in lower Manhattan), where he pursued the life of a free-spirited (make that responsibility-free) artist.

My dad was also big drinker, and growing up I was constantly rescuing him from scrapes. I often felt like the adult in the relationship. I spent a good part of my teen years and early twenties saving him, and it's no surprise that I was attracted to women who needed my help. My friends used to joke that I enjoyed my Svengali-like role, molding women who were financially, emotionally, and intellectually dependent on me. But really, my choices belied a deeper fear of abandonment.

I'm not suggesting that everyone on the dating treadmill is a candidate for psychoanalysis but I do think that if you reflect

upon your childhood, you'll recognize patterns that repeat themselves in your romantic life—sometimes for better, often for worse. Usually, these patterns are acted upon unconsciously until an experience forces us to take stock of ourselves. For me, it came through creative writing. In college, I'd wanted to be a playwright, and my dramas were filled with anger and rage. But I was never writing about myself, at least consciously—I was always creating "characters."

Finally, I had the guts to write about my relationship with my father in a play entitled *Straight Man*. I'd chosen that title because it occurred to me while writing that I'd always played the straight sidekick to my father's larger-than-life personality, at the cost of my own emotional growth. I cried my way through writing that play but it allowed me to confront painful issues that I'd always been too afraid to deal with.

When I finished the play, I felt transformed. I was a different person, and yet everything around me was still the same: my job, my apartment, my dancer-fianceé. It was all so claustrophobic, and I knew I had to act fast.

There's a poem by the German poet Rilke that helped me understand my situation and gave me the impetus to make a change. Entitled "The Panther," its few verses depict the sad life of a wildcat captured in the jungle and reduced to the confinement of a zoo. Here are a couple of stanzas:

> *His tired gaze—from passing endless bars—*
> *has turned into a vacant stare which nothing holds.*
> *To him there seem to be a thousand bars,*
> *and out beyond these bars exists no world.*

*But sometimes the curtains of his eyelids part,*
*the pupils of his eyes dilate as images*
*of past encounters enter while through his limbs*
*a tension strains in silence*
*only to cease to be, to die within his heart.*

I felt like that panther, trapped in a cage of my own design. (It's hard to see the bars, especially when you've built them yourself.) But now I was experiencing the impulse of life and I knew I couldn't let it die within my heart.

And so I left the cage of my former life, not knowing what was out there, but not willing to give up and marry someone I didn't truly love with all my heart and soul. As it turned out, real love was waiting for me; in fact, you could even say it was looking for me. (Not only did my future wife live two blocks away from me, we worked in the same office space, and she was best friends with my best friend's best friend.) Small world, huh? What's even more strange was that there were a number of occasions when we'd been in the same room with each other, and yet when we met on our first date, neither of us recognized the other. It didn't matter that we'd been separated by a matter of inches a few times in the past—it might as well have been a million miles because we weren't ready for love. Well, I wasn't anyway.

I'll let my wife speak for herself. . . .

*D*on't hate me because I'm married. Deep down, I still feel like Bridget Jones. I pinch myself every day over the fact that I found love. As a feminist, I definitely don't view marriage as the be-all-end-all, and it's certainly not for everyone. But it's definitely something I always wanted. If it's something you've always wanted too and you're frustrated at the lack of marital prospects out there, perhaps my story will give you hope. My sexual history can be counted on one hand—a hand missing a few fingers, to be exact. I'm one of those terminally nice girls who always wound up as a girlfriend. Even the times I tried to have a one-night stand evolved into five-year relationships.

There are a few reasons for this: First, my mother taught me not to need a man. Period. Second, I'm a specific type: small, short hair, quirky. Guys either thought of me as a little boy or the girl of their dreams. Third, I have an all-or-nothing libido: Either I am totally, hopelessly, psychotically in love with you or I'm not.

And if I'm not, I can't kiss, slow dance, or receive your foot rub, let alone sleep with you. I'd tried on several occasions to be a slut but I failed. In high school, I had a fantastic boyfriend, followed by a terrific college boyfriend, followed by a post-college hookup friendship that chugged on for five middling years until it died a slow death.

In every case, I was the one to break it off. I felt that I had made smart, careful decisions and figured that all good things come to an end. Like Estella in *Great Expectations,* I was safe in my smug cocoon. Young, healthy, with great friends and a dream job, I might like a guy, love him even, but *need* him? Not so much. I felt immune to heartache—that is, until the day I met the English guy. [Cue dark clouds, a crackle of lightning, creepy organ music.] Let's call him the Chippy. The Chippy was my undoing. Every woman should have a Chippy in her life: a person who decimates her, humiliates her, makes her suffer bestial amounts of pain. I'm sure you have yours. You just might not realize how good he actually is for you.

The Chippy was the best thing that could have happened to me because the experience forced me to grow up. By meeting Mr. Terribly Wrong, I was able to recognize Mr. Finally Right.

And here's the (abridged) saga:

The Chippy and I crossed paths at an Irish bar in lower Manhattan one fateful fall evening. Boyish and witty, he looked like a young Paul McCartney. He had one of those hipster rooster haircuts that, along with the accent, had enabled British men to seduce American women since Mick Jagger was in his prime.

We flirted sarcastically the night we met and fell into a casual, no-strings relationship. There was intense chemistry but, hey, no need to get all serious here. He was my first non-boyfriend. The "I'm just a girlfriend" spell was finally broken. Then four months in, he told me he was moving back to the United Kingdom. What aphrodisiac is more powerful than something you cannot have?

I showed up at his going-away barbeque in a hot black dress bearing marshmallows. Suddenly, it became important that he stay. The English BBQ consisted of a few pizzas and a lot of beer, with no grill in sight, so we roasted the marshmallows over his stovetop. It was there that I decided I was in love.

Up on his building's rooftop that night, he grabbed my face and professed his love for me. The New York skyline was a blanket of twinkling candles. My dress blew up around my legs as we kissed. For a moment, I was Annie Hall.

Things were going well until I made a fatal mistake, one that would send him scrambling back to England, where he would disappear into a sea of fish and chips leaving me holding nothing but the greasy paper. I told him that I felt exactly the same way. And just like that, things unraveled. Once the chase was up and I requited his feelings, he lost interest. I went from being the love of his life to the stalker of his nightmares.

But it wasn't all me. A dishonest trader of affection, he continued to lay it on thick and then take it all back. He would breeze into town unannounced and over dinner confess he couldn't live without me, only to tell me the next morning that he was sorry but he had a girlfriend.

I became undone, turning myself into one of those needy, pining girls my mother warned me about.

It was the least significant relationship I'd ever had, so why was I not getting over him?

It took an agonizing four years to realize that the Chippy was a figment of my imagination, that he was my imaginary boyfriend.

I concocted a superficial fantasy that was based mainly around an accent and a stylish haircut, and I became addicted to this fantasy. The man I had created had very little to do with the actual person who was making me miserable. What I had from him were a few sassy e-mails, an occasional spicy hookup, and a few sweet moments. Not much to really go on. But *Trainspotting* had just come out and musicwise, the British were invading pop culture once again. Urged on by Ewan McGregor, Irvine Welsh, Damien Hirst, and those damn Oasis brothers, I filled in the rest.

I held on to this fantasy like a stubborn little pit bull. I pined, I whined, I drank too much whiskey. I went to psychics and astrologers, anyone who would give me a shred of hope. I went to the bars we used to frequent and ended up crying in the bathroom. I would write e-mails just to let him know that: "Dude, I am so over you." But, of course, we both knew I was lying.

I listened to the Beatles and kissed English strangers with bad teeth. I stopped telling my friends that I still thought about him because after four years, it was becoming schizophrenic.

As crazy as my story may sound, I believe a lot of women go through this. We women have rich fantasy lives. When we are with the wrong man and he is clearly lacking the qualities we want in a partner, we gladly supply them for him. We fill in the blanks instead of realizing he's wrong to begin with.

The most important quality a man must have, first and foremost, is that he is interested in us. We forget this; we hang on with hope and denial. And when that man, who is wrong for us anyway, loses interest, our egos kick in and all the weepy, bad behavior spirals into self-destruction and humiliation.

So how did I finally get over the bloody bastard? My epiphany occurred in an astrologer's hovel. A preternatural sprite, she is the person who saved my life. Surrounded by dusty crystals and a yapping Yorkie, she leaned into the table, snapped off the tape recorder, and said, "Why are you doing this to yourself?"

I sat back and thought about it.

Why *am* I doing this?

And it dawned on me . . . the whole time I worried about why he didn't like me, I forgot to ask myself whether or not I liked him.

I didn't actually like this person.

Ha!

I tried to imagine what we would look like as an elderly married couple. Would we be rocking out to Radiohead in our wheelchairs? Would he still have enough hair to be fashionably styled? Would I still think his beer-over-indulgence was cute? What the hell was I thinking?

And just like that, the flame was finally snuffed out.

I came to understand that commitment-phobes are not only unable to commit to "yes," they are also incapable of committing to "no." They keep the door open, giving their partners false hope.

From there, I reflected on my goals. I came to the realization that I needed to become my best self in order to attract the kind of guy I would want to marry. If I wanted someone truly fabulous, I had better become truly fabulous first.

So, I cleaned house. I cut it off cold turkey with the Chippy and my other crutch, the post-college hookup friend. I started sticking to a three-times-a-week yoga schedule. I joined a writing group. My directing career became my focus, and it started taking off.

I stopped searching for men everywhere. I went out and started enjoying my life. Single or not, I was going to be happy. When I did meet a guy, I was careful to watch out for red flags. If a guy let me know he wasn't available, I damn well took his word for it.

I did my homework and saved myself potential heartbreak a dozen times. I can't say it was easy. There were too many nights where I was the fifth wheel. Too many people asking, "What is wrong with you? How can you still be single? Are you too picky?" From grandmothers, to dental hygienists to married friends, society loves to pick apart the single girl.

"Such a pretty girl . . . I don't understand it." I remember getting a massage and being surprised to feel tears rolling down my cheeks. I hadn't been touched in so long.

And about a year or so later, I reluctantly agreed to a blind date. I said yes because my friend promised me this date would tell me a fantastic ghost story and I just love a good ghost story. I was intrigued but wary. Ian was the best friend of the childhood best friend of my childhood friend's best friend (the point is, we had a reference point, however oblique). Still, I tried to back out a few times. I was sure it would be a disaster.

Over the phone, we realized we had met a number of times—we lived a few blocks away from each other and went to the same bookstores and cafés. We had even gone to a play together with a group of friends and gone for drinks after. We were sure we would recognize each other on our date.

We arranged to meet at a corner on the Upper West Side. I remember walking across the street that night, seeing Ian from a distance, and not recognizing him. I had no idea that I was heading toward my future husband.

What I do remember, however, are his shoes. I remember loafers, black and shiny, with tassels. A huge "no." Ian swears he has never even owned a pair of tasseled shoes. I remember tassels.

We now laugh about this, but pre-Chippy, the tassels might have been a deal-breaker.

But as the dinner progressed I found Ian to be charming, attractive, and articulate. His extensive vocabulary gave me a boner. I remember thinking, *This is a man I can learn from.* There is nothing sexier than that.

We discovered that we had both been reading the same book at the same time, F. Scott Fitzgerald's *Tender Is the Night.* We shared a love of literature, theater, practical jokes, and scary movies. We had the same perverse sense of humor. I liked the way he smelled.

Yet I remained skeptical.

I'd like to say it was love at first sight but it wasn't. Love at first sight is a false conceit; people confuse it for chemistry, which, while important, is just a fraction of what makes a relationship work.

I was so entrenched in my career and so used to things not working out that the love of my life was right under my nose and I almost missed him. I had swung so far into independence that I almost blew it. I had mistaken the lack of drama ("Will he call? Does he like me?") for a lack of passion.

Rather than an instant heat, where the risk for burning out was high, our relationship was a slow, steady flame that eventually came to a boil. When it works, it's easy. He wants to see you. You want to see him. There are no doubts, excuses, maybes, or buts. You don't have to analyze the relationship. There are no games.

When I think of the efforts I made, strapping on sexy shoes and skimpy outfits in the dead of winter, hauling my butt downtown every night, going to every art opening, concert, party, and reading, just in case true love was waiting, it kills me to think that he was right there in my neighborhood, two blocks away, at the same parties, even at the same dinner table.

I'm not sure if I believe in fate but it seems that some force kept putting the two of us together even though we kept ignoring the signs.

When we women complain that there are no good single men left, we may be doing so with half-closed eyes. Or are we looking for the wrong criteria? For me, it was a haircut and a pair of shoes but many women will write off a guy if he is not tall, or broad-shouldered, or dark-haired, or possessing any of a hundred other shallow attributes.

As our relationship unfolded, I was traveling a lot for business and there were weeks when Ian didn't hear from me. When we did see each other, it was incredible. But while I was away, I concentrated on my career. Looking back, I realize that this was a form of self-protection, a way of managing my hopes. I was not playing hard to get; I was simply not available.

But six months into the relationship, I (finally) fell in love. Lucky for me, Ian was patient.

We were married a year later. There were excerpts from *Tender Is the Night* in our vows, and fried chicken and cotton candy at our reception. It was a magical night but it was simply that: a night.

Six years later, our marriage is incredibly strong, passionate, and happy. It is a relationship grounded in reality and respect. Of course, there have been tough moments but my long-term single-girl status makes me appreciative of what I have. I know what the other side feels like. Last year, we had a son, Owen, and the most mundane and simplest moments spent together are easily my life's most blissful. This is what it's all about.

So what do I want to say when I see packs of single women eyeballing my little family on the street? The package wrapping your future husband comes in might not seem perfect to you at first glance but the stuff inside can surpass your greatest fantasies.

Also, you never know when marriage is going to sneak up and bite you in the ass. So be ready.

Postscript:

Ian chose his own shoes for our wedding: a pair of chocolate brown Jimmy Choos, fabulous and tassel-free.

A final comment from Ian:

In closing, I need to tell you that my courtship of Lisa nearly killed me. She'll tell you that she wasn't playing hard to get, she simply *was* hard to get. Either way, it was one hell of a chase. Or, as I like to call it, an "exquisite torture"—long bouts of uncertainty, frustration, and longing punctuated by brief moments of togetherness that left me craving more. In that in-between state, I couldn't sleep, I couldn't eat, I couldn't think straight. My friends told me to give her up, that she clearly wasn't "into me."

But in my own seemingly cool but secretly desperate fashion I kept pursuing, and the chase brought out the best in me. It forced me to believe in myself—to believe that I was deserving and worthy of someone who was so terrific and to have the confidence to persist in my quest. Today, Lisa is my life partner and I'm grateful for the love we share. Just this morning I was watching *Sesame Street* with our seventeen-month-old son and Big Bird was singing the "one of these things doesn't belong" song. And I realized that love is sort of like that song—you need to know what belongs and what doesn't but you can only do that by really knowing yourself. All of my life I had settled for people who didn't belong. It took a while but I finally found the one who truly does belong. And if I can do it, so can you.

And P.S.: I don't care what Lisa says, I've never, *ever* owned a pair of shoes with tassels.

*acknowledgments*

*I* am indebted to Judith Regan for her enthusiasm, vision, and personal commitment to this book. Some of the best times during the writing were my conversations with Judith, and I'm grateful for her attentiveness.

My gratitude also goes out to Cassie Jones for her responsiveness, insight, and editorial stewardship.

Thanks to Amy Baron for getting the word out; everyone in sales, marketing, and publicity at ReganBooks; and all those behind the scenes who embraced the spirit of hustle on this project.

Many thanks to *New York* magazine columnist Amy Sohn (*My Old Man*), for lending her humor and intelligence to the preface. Her columns and books have always helped me to interpret the cultural zeitgeist and to laugh along the way.

I owe a considerable debt of gratitude to Peter Hyman (*The Reluctant Metrosexual: Dispatches from an Almost Hip Life*), a truly first-rate writer and journalist. Peter worked diligently with me through every page of this book, adding comedic flourish, literary flair, and cultural insights.

And to my supertalented friends and stand-in editors, Sue Rosenstock and Delia Peretta, who read every word of the manuscript and never failed to offer insights and suggestions. I can't thank them enough for the generous bestowal of their time and talent. Sue, Delia, now it's your turn to get me your pages!

To my friend Adena Halpern, thank you for opening your treasure trove of dating stories.

And a special thanks to all the friends, patients, colleagues, and "women and men of America" who shared their stories and opinions on the subject of their singlehood. Thank you for letting me change your names and share your experiences.

And finally, to my wife, Lisa, a life partner in every sense of the word. Thank you for inspiring me to raise my standards and providing me with the love I reached for.